GOD SPEAKS IN LETTERS

OF

ETERNITY

ANTHONY A EDDY

Copyright and Publishing

© 2019 by BookWhip Publishing.

All rights reserved. No part of this publication may be reproduced, stored in a retrieval system or transmitted in any way by any means, electronic, mechanical, photocopy, recording or otherwise without the prior permission of the author except as provided by USA copyright law.

Soft Cover ISBN: 978-1-951469-15-3
Hard Cover ISBN: 978-1-951469-49-8
Ebook ISBN: 978-1-951469-50-4

5. "GOD Speaks in Letters of Eternity"

To order additional copies of this book, contact:
Bookwhip
1-855-339-3589
https://www.bookwhip.com

Cover design, Manuscript Content and Layout, Conceptual Related Imagery and titling texts, ©® Copyright May 2014, Jan 2016, Apr 2018, 2017, 2019 by The Advent Charitable Trust, CC45056, Hamilton, New Zealand. All rights reserved worldwide.

www.thewebsiteofthelord.org.nz

Prepared on a 27in iMac™© with the use of Nisus®© Writer Pro. All trademarks™ and intellectual rights remain the property of their respective owners.

Dedication

"The Spirit of the Lord GOD *is* upon Me, Because the LORD has anointed Me To preach good tidings to the poor; He has sent Me to heal the brokenhearted, To proclaim liberty to the captives, And the opening of the prison to *those who are* bound; To proclaim the acceptable year of the LORD, And the day of vengeance of our God; To comfort all who mourn, To console those who mourn in Zion, To give them beauty for ashes, The oil of joy for mourning, The garment of praise for the spirit of heaviness; That they may be called trees of righteousness, The planting of the LORD, that He may be glorified."

Isaiah 61:1-3

Scripture taken from the New King James Version of The Bible.
Copyright © 1982 by Thomas Nelson, Inc.
Used by permission. All rights reserved.

I again have very real cause for gratitude in offering the preparation of this, His fifth, book also into His care.

To our God of love, of justice, of redemption
who is very interested in all we do
and in our achieving our return home.

For He alone is worthy of the devotion of man.

Acknowledgements

This is the time to thank Adrienne, my dear wife, for her support and interest, for her oversight and care, for her forbearance and her love, as these books have been coming forth into the existence of man.

This book is as God would have it be— both in its content and in its presentation. I offer it to God as a love gift from within His Grace; and thank Him for His unfading patience with me.

May God our loving Father, Jesus Christ His Son, together with The Holy Spirit as our counsellor— bless and favour his family in all they do and bring to pass in the growth and development of His kingdom here in New Zealand and around the world. Marana tha— O Lord, come!

*All donated funds received go in their entirety to
The Advent Charitable Trust, unless directed by a donor,
in order to further,
the scope and the objectives of this charity's christian call
within The Kingdom of God.*

The banner of the kingdom was first flown as a flag at
10.30am on Monday, 1st September 2008
in Hamilton, New Zealand.

*The banner of the kingdom was first flown as His flag on His church
in the village of* **Burripalem**
*near Tenali, Andhra Pradesh, in India,
on*
Sunday, 31st July 2011
*in unity with
Reaching Forward Ministries of Tenali, Andhra Pradesh, India.*

GOD Speaks in

On that close to His heart for the attention span of man;
so man may fully understand the eternal message;
as spelt out for his attention within his day:
to accumulate the knowledge building—
into his preparation for his time:
with his Loving Living God.

Letters of Eternity

These letters are compilations scribed in obedience to God;
testify of His great willingness to speak to man,
in this day, at the closure of an age;
with an invitation to inspect
the table of His menu:
as laid for man.

Anthony A Eddy
(Scribe)

Contents— Order Received

(2, 3, 4 ...) Denotes following items with a similar or same name as earlier ones

Title: God Speaks in Letters of Eternity	I
Copyright and Publishing	II
Dedication	III
Acknowledgements	IV
God Speaks on His Eternity	V
Content— Ordered Index	VI
Content— Alphabetical Index	VIII
Content— Category Index	X
Prelude	XII
My Letters From The Son	XIII
My Letter Especially to You. Yes, to YOU!	XVI
Coming Presentations	XVIII
Stepping Stone of Mortality	XX
Introduction	XXIII

01. Visiting of Megiddon	1
02. Outreach of My People	3
03. Decoration of The Heavens	5
04. Wastelands of God	8
05. Inside of The Eyelids	10
06. Veins and Arteries	12
07. Waterways of God	14
08. Vagrancy of The Youth	16
09. Vacuum of Space	18
10. Viceroy of India	20
11. Disappointments of God	22
12. Clavicles of Grace	24
13. Land of Goshen	26
14. Eternity of God	29
15. Camaraderie of The Soul	31
16. Faith of Man	33
17. Welcome of The Centuries	36
18. Means of Man	38
19. Lumps of Clay	41
20. Location of Man	43
21. Incubators of Man	45
22. Embarking on A Journey	47
23. Seeping of The Blood	49
24. My Children of The World	51
25. Storm of The Wealth of Man	53
26. Crossing of The Threshold	56
27. Writings of God	57
28. Sky Signs of God	59
29. Boundaries of The Earth	62
30. Capacity of Man	64
31. Love Note to My Children	66
32. Faith Filled Faithful Servants	67
33. God of Man	70
34. Scenery of God Abroad	72
35. Awakening of My People	74
36. Way Stations of The Lord	77
37. Twisting of the Tongue of Man	79
38. Sealing of The Temple	81
39. Compulsion of The Soul	83
40. Non-vindictiveness of God	85
41. Sacrifice of Self	86
42. Grain of Wood	88
43. Stones of The Earth	89
44. Wind of My Spirit (2)	93
45. Misery of Man (2)	95
46. Dependencies of Man	98
47. Glory on Man	99
48. Behold The Bride of Christ	101
49. My Relationship With Man	103
50. Washing of The Clothes	106
51. Game Hunters of The Earth	108
52. Magnificence of God	110
53. Voice of Man	112
54. Joy of The Lord	114

55. Vanguard of My Spirit	116
56. Firestorm of My Spirit	118
57. Template for The Future	120
58. Home of Godly Wisdom	122
59. Wool of My Sheep	124
60. New Prince is Born	126
61. Friendships of Man	127
62. Aberrations of Man	129
63. Wonderment of Eternity	131
64. Doorway of Mercy	133
65. Presence of Man	135
66. Restlessness of Man	137
67. Resilience of Man	139
68. Variance of Man	141
69. Choices of Man	143
70. Surprises of Man	145
71. Perspicacity of Man	148
72. Wayward Wind	150
73. Smaller Becomes Better	152
74. Journeying of Man	154
75. Generosity of Man	156
76. Escape of Man	158
77. Vanity of Man (2)	160
78. Son Shines	162
79. Beyond The Grave of Man	164

Appendix:	169
Prologue: The Hubble Cross	*170*
Journaling and Notes (1-2)	*171*
About the Scribe	*173*
Epilogue: Laminin	*174*
His Books 2 and 3 Reviews	*175*
End-time Psalms of God	177

Contents— Alphabetical

(2, 3, 4 ...) Denotes following items with a similar or same name as earlier ones

Title: God Speaks in Letters of Eternity	I
Copyright and Publishing	II
Dedication	III
Acknowledgements	IV
God Speaks on His Eternity	V
Content— Ordered Index	VI
Content— Alphabetical Index	VIII
Content— Category Index	X
Prelude	XII
My Letters From The Son	XIII
My Letter Especially to You. Yes, to YOU!	XVI
Coming Presentations	XVIII
Stepping Stone of Mortality	XX
Introduction	XXIII

A
62 Aberrations of Man	129
35 Awakening of My People	74

B
48 Behold The Bride of Christ	101
79 Beyond The Grave of Man	164
29 Boundaries of The Earth	62

C
15 Camaraderie of The Soul	31
30 Capacity of Man	64
69 Choices of Man	143
12 Clavicles of Grace	24
Coming Presentations	XVIII
39 Compulsion of The Soul	83
26 Crossing of The Threshold	56

D
03 Decoration of The Heavens	5
46 Dependencies of Man	98
11 Disappointments of God	22
64 Doorway of Mercy	133

E
22 Embarking on A Journey	47
76 Escape of Man	158
14 Eternity of God	29

F
16 Faith of Man	33
32 Faith Filled Faithful Servants	67
56 Firestorm of My Spirit	118
61 Friendships of Man	127

G
51 Game Hunters of The Earth	108
75 Generosity of Man	156
47 Glory on Man	99
33 God of Man	70
42 Grain of Wood	88

H
58 Home of Godly Wisdom	122

I
21 Incubators of Man	45
05 Inside of The Eyelids	10

J
74 Journeying of Man	154
54 Joy of The Lord	114

L
13 Land of Goshen	26
20 Location of Man	43
31 Love Note to My Children	66
19 Lumps of Clay	41

M
52 Magnificence of God	110
18 Means of Man	38
45 Misery of Man (2)	95

24 My Children of The World	51	06 Veins and Arteries	12
My Letter Especially to You!	XVI	10 Viceroy of India	20
My Letters From The Son	XIII	01 Visiting of Megiddon	1
49 My Relationship With Man	103	53 Voice of Man	112

N

60 New Prince is Born	126		
40 Non-vindictiveness of God	85		

W

50 Washing of The Clothes	106
04 Wastelands of God	8
07 Waterways of God	14
36 Way Stations of The Lord	77
72 Wayward Wind	150
17 Welcome of The Centuries	36
44 Wind of My Spirit (2)	93
63 Wonderment of Eternity	131
59 Wool of My Sheep	124
27 Writings of God	57

O

02 Outreach of My people	3

P

71 Perspicacity of Man	148
65 Presence of Man	135

R

67 Resilience of Man	139
66 Restlessness of Man	137

S

41 Sacrifice of Self	86
34 Scenery of God Abroad	72
38 Sealing of The Temple	81
23 Seeping of The Blood	49
28 Sky Signs of God	59
73 Smaller Becomes Better	152
78 Son Shines	162
Stepping Stone of Mortality	XX
43 Stones of The Earth	89
25 Storm of The Wealth of Man	53
70 Surprises of Man	145

Appendix:	169
Prologue: The Hubble Cross	*170*
Journaling and Notes (1-2)	*171*
About the Scribe	*173*
Epilogue: Laminin	*174*
His Books 2 and 3 Reviews	*175*
End-time Psalms of God	177

T

57 Template for The Future	120
37 Twisting of the Tongue of Man	79

V

09 Vacuum of Space	18
08 Vagrancy of The Youth	16
55 Vanguard of My Spirit	116
77 Vanity of Man (2)	160
68 Variance of Man	141

Contents— Category

(2, 3, 4 ...) Denotes following items with a similar or same name as earlier ones

Title: God Speaks in Letters of Eternity	I
Copyright and Publishing	II
Dedication	III
Acknowledgements	IV
God Speaks on His Eternity	V
Content— Ordered Index	VI
Content— Alphabetical Index	VIII
Content— Category Index	X
Prelude	XII
My Letters From The Son	XIII
My Letter Especially to You. Yes, to YOU!	XVI
Coming Presentations	XVIII
Stepping Stone of Mortality	XX
Introduction	XXIII

Encouragement (11)

15. Camaraderie of The Soul	31
16. Faith of Man	33
19. Lumps of Clay	41
43. Stones of The Earth	89
54. Joy of The Lord	114
59. Wool of My Sheep	124
68. Variance of Man	141
70. Surprises of Man	145
73. Smaller Becomes Better	152
75. Generosity of Man	156
My Letter Especially to You. Yes, to YOU!	XVI

Eternity Beckoning (9)

03. Decoration of The Heavens	5
09. Vacuum of Space	18
12. Clavicles of Grace	24
14. Eternity of God	29
24. My Children of The World	51
34. Scenery of God Abroad	72
41. Sacrifice of Self	86
63. Wonderment of Eternity	131
79. Beyond The Grave of Man	164

Freewill of Man (4)

18. Means of Man	38
29. Boundaries of The Earth	62
57. Template for The Future	120
69. Choices of Man	143

My Counsel (17)

07. Waterways of God	14
11. Disappointments of God	22
13. Land of Goshen	26
25. Storm of The Wealth of Man	53
37. Twisting of the Tongue of Man	79
38. Sealing of The Temple	81
39. Compulsion of The Soul	83
45. Misery of Man (2)	95
50. Washing of The Clothes	106
51. Game Hunters of The Earth	108
60. New Prince is Born	126
62. Aberrations of Man	129
65. Presence of Man	135
66. Restlessness of Man	137
72. Wayward Wind	150
76. Escape of Man	158
77. Vanity of Man (2)	160

My Creation (6)

04. Wastelands of God	8
21. Incubators of Man	45
23. Seeping of The Blood	49
26. Crossing of The Threshold	56
28. Sky Signs of God	59
42. Grain of Wood	88

My Grace (3)

35. Awakening of My People	74
49. My Relationship With Man	103
Stepping Stone of Mortality	*XX*

My Harvest (5)

02. Outreach of My People	3
06. Veins and Arteries	12
32. Faith Filled Faithful Servants	67
46. Dependencies of Man	98
55. Vanguard of My Spirit	116

My Kingdom on Earth (3)

10. Viceroy of India	20
53. Voice of Man	112
61. Friendships of Man	127

My Love (5)

20. Location of Man	43
22. Embarking on A Journey	47
30. Capacity of Man	64
31. Love Note to My Children	66
58. Home of Godly Wisdom	122

My Return (4)

17. Welcome of The Centuries	36
48. Behold The Bride of Christ	101
64. Doorway of Mercy	133
Coming Presentations	XVIII

Preparation (6)

01. Visiting of Megiddon	1
05. Inside of The Eyelids	10
08. Vagrancy of The Youth	16
47. Glory on Man	99
67. Resilience of Man	139
74. Journeying of Man	154

The Cross (1)

36. Way Stations of The Lord	77

The Trinity (8)

27. Writings of God	57
33. God of Man	70
40. Non-vindictiveness of God	85
44. Wind of My Spirit (2)	93
52. Magnificence of God	110
56. Firestorm of My Spirit	118
78. Son Shines	162
My Letters From The Son	XIII

Tongues (1)

71. Perspicacity of Man	148

Appendix:	169
Prologue: The Hubble Cross	*170*
Journaling and Notes (1-2)	*171*
About the Scribe	*173*
Epilogue: Laminin	*174*
His Books 2 and 3 Reviews	*175*
End-time Psalms of God	177

Prelude

This book speaks with an emphasis on eternity in a series of letters from The Son— delivered By God for reading within the attention span of man.

Each letter is worthy of the thought of man, is worthy of its message being understood, is worthy of the implications brought before the life styles of man.

These letters impart knowledge, bring encouragement, confirm an open Heaven in the presence of The Living God.

These books are each a consecutive part in an overall grand vision positioned to give voice to these declarations within the will of God— for these days— the end-time prior to His return.

The end-time is to see conflicts on massive scales becoming evident in nature and evident within the attitudes and relationships of man.

Sooner or later man, in his wisdom, will be found on his knees before His God— positioned just below the swinging of the sword.

Agapé,
Anthony,
His servant and His scribe.
Hamilton, New Zealand.

My Letters From The Son

"I,
    The Lord,
        see man from far,
        see man from closeup,
        see man as he wishes,
        see man as he is.

I,
    The Lord,
        of his creation,
            know man very well—
                both in his failings and in his successes;
                both in his sliding down the slippery slope of Satan and in his reaching
                                            for the stars of God;
                both in the worship of his gods and in the devotion to his God.

I,
    The Lord,
        am not surprised by man—
            either in the depths of his iniquities or in the heights of his altruism.

I,
    The Lord,
        commend man for his faith,
        rebuke man for his carnality;
        encourage man to walk the road of discipleship,
        discourage man who would follow the enticements of Satan;
        extend My hand in fellowship,
        withdraw My hand upon refusal.

I,
    The Lord,
        would rather willingly honour the freewill of man,
        than being entailed to proceed in respect of that freewill.

I,
    The Lord,
        dictate this letter to all those upon The Earth,
            My book of My eternity,
            My book of My disclosures,
            My book of My encouragements:
                      with an invitation born of Grace—
            for the acceptance by man in these days of dwindling freedom;
                in these days of increasing distancing as the secular attempts to frustrate
                                            the plans of God.

I,
- The Lord,
  - offer a life of understanding,
  - offer a life as promised,
  - offer a life of no regrets,
  - offer a life of close companionship,
  - offer a life of an enduring relationship,
  - offer a life with integrity of purpose in the walk with truth.

I,
- The Lord,
  - know the present from the past,
  - know the future from the present,
  - know the thoughts and will of man,
  - know the granting of man's freewill which brings recrimination upon the head
    of God:
    - when man would move the responsibility from his own.

I,
- The Lord,
  - can read the heart of man for intent—
    - as it comes before Me as an open book.

I,
- The Lord,
  - can purchase and redeem,
  - can locate and salve,
  - can offer and uphold.

I,
- The Lord,
  - can mend and heal,
  - can guide and teach,
  - can disciple and instruct.

I,
- The Lord,
  - can speak and be heard,
  - can issue and confirm,
  - can call and task:
    - from the sanctum of God—
    - from The Temple of My Spirit,
    - from within the glove of the spirit and the soul—
      - the confines of My Saints.

I,
- The Lord,
  - speak a welcome to man with a willing spirit:

        yet adrift within the wilderness of the secular;
        yet lost within the jungles of the cities;
        yet distraught within the fields of temptation on the plains which border
                the deserts of despair.

I,
    The Lord,
        offer living water to the thirsty,
        offer victory to the fallen,
        offer credence to the liars, offer
        restitution to the thieves, offer
        new life to the squanderers.

I,
    The Lord,
        offer Grace to all who stand in conviction of My Spirit,
            who desire to make all well.

I,
    The Lord,
        present this,
            My Book of Letters:
                to the silenced spirit,
                to the broken soul,
                to the captured body—
                      that freedom may break forth as the leaves in spring,
            to blossom with the sun in the unending days of summer—
                      with the slaking of the thirst—
            with the restoring of the body soul and spirit."

Gratefully received from The Lord for use in this, the front of His book five.

My Content Study Aid

_____
_____
_____
_____
_____
_____
_____
_____

My Letter Especially to You. Yes, to YOU!

"Do you know I live for ever?
Do you know I care for you?

Do you know I'd like to take you with Me—
                to places you have never seen—
                to the places here on Earth;
                to the centres among the heavens?

Do you know that I love you very much—
    even though you may have never met Me?

    Even though you may have thought I did not exist:
        may have listened to the rumour mill to draw your
                                            own conclusions?

Do you know Me in relationship,
                or via a ship of state?
Do you seek Me so to find Me,
                or turn away despaired?

Are you too busy to discuss your being of existence?
    Would you like to choose your destination?
        Or follow with the crowd that cares not where it's going?

Are you a good listener who would love to hear the truth?
        Or one who carries on with life and knows not where it ends?

Do you know I knew your spirit long before your birth?
Do you know I knew your grandparents when things were that much simpler and love
                                                        was to the fore?
Do you know I walked with Abraham and have watched the nations grow?
Do you know I am alive and well and remember all which has been written down?

Do you know I would seek your hand to hold it high in victory,
                to take you on a journey,
                to disciple you in truth,
                to lead you home to become a child of God
                                      within My family?

For My sheep know The Good Shepherd and listen to My voice,
        can know the wonder of discovery and find great joy
                                        within the journey home,
    can come to know great faith and to receive The Gifts of God.

For My sheep are each in possession of A Temple in which My Spirit dwells.

    I love you with all My heart.
        In deed I do!
            Invite Me.
                Learn of Me.
                    And I will stay with you if wanted.
                      Agapé for ever,
                        Jesus."

My Content Study Aid

The Coming Presentations

"The coming authority for man is one of Righteousness and justice for all,
        is one of Truth with the forsaking of the lies,
        is one of Peace and growth within the family of God,
        is one where eyes are on The Multitudes for when a hand
                is raised intentionally.

The coming of a king is with the groundwork well laid,
        is with an awareness of the time and season,
            of the age and epoch,
              of the heavenly attention seen to be falling on
                  The Earth.

The coming of a king is not a frequent happening,
        is about to change the circumstances of man,
        is about to bring,
        is about to replace,
        is about to oversee the better as it supplants the worse.

The coming of a king sees a kingdom close at hand,
        sees a kingdom waiting in the wings,
        sees a kingdom about to enter centre stage—
    where the stage hands and the builders have all been willingly supplied.

The coming of a king awaits the fullness of preparation,
        awaits The Bridal Dress of presentation readied for proceedings,
        awaits the discernment of My people found in their robes
                of righteousness,
        awaits The Multitudes at large as knowledge is assembled.

The coming of the throne of governance dispenses the decrees in affirmation,
            instates the edicts building nationhood,
            resolves the disputes of the past,
            settles the infractions of expectations.

The coming of the courtiers attends to matters of inheritance,
        attends to causes of complaint,
        attends to the remedies for injustice,
        brings the righting to negate the wrongs.

The coming of authority presents an opportunity to shine,
        approves the star-dusting from the angels,
        welcomes the songs of children,
        affirms each dwelling place as set within eternity.

The coming of peace removes contestants attentive only to their wants,

    removes the cycling of despair without an end in sight,
    removes the seeking of publicity for the getters of attention—
        living both in pride and selfishness,
    removes the dissatisfied and the snarling to a distance
        deemed acceptable.

The Inaugural Banner flies on high in presence.
The Colours of The King are asserted with a claim.
The Fanfares of The Kingdom flow and ebb with the currency of the ceremonies.
The Anthem of The King announces in regalia,
    with full honour,
    the seating on The Great White Throne.

The future of man is certified according to his imprint with freewill,
    according to one born of relationship and trust,
    according to what was ever swept under the mat of entry,
    according to that whose presence was abhorred.

The future of My people is assured of,
    and welcome to,
        life within eternity,
        life within a garden,
        the viewing of creation,
        the learning and establishing of thought patterning—
            within the university of God."

My Content Study Aid

_____
_____
_____
_____
_____
_____
_____
_____
_____
_____
_____
_____

A Stepping Stone of Mortality

"The future of man is unveiling within The Will of God,
                within the close attention of his God,
                within The Future Edicts of The Lord—
                              awaiting their time on Earth,
                within the panorama before the eyes and ears of man,
                within the future scope of man able and willing to consent.

The future of man is dependent on his knowledge,
                is a measure of his wisdom,
                is the status of his freewill history,
                is his willingness to change when a journey is partially completed.

The future of man is to receive a letter from God,
                is to receive the fare as set upon The Table of The Lord,
                is to receive the love and honour due a compliant child of God,
                is to receive the welcome home extended to the prodigal sons of man.

The future of man is within his destiny of choice,
                is within The Family of God,
                is within the garden of God,
                is within the creation of God.

The coming letters to man are as in My fifth book of The End-time Psalms of God,
                are as in the time frame of disclosures,
                are as in the acceptance of The Multitudes,
                are as in the preparedness of My people awaiting My Return.

The coming letters to man are of expectations for eternity,
                are of The Need for Preparation,
                are for the need to use the eternal gifts available,
                are about the need to plan and to conform—
                              to righteousness and truth.

The coming letters are about to hit the bookstalls of man,
                are about to become The Centres of Attention,
                are about to preside over discussions of a destiny,
                are about to resolve the significance of lightness from the darkness.

The coming letters emanate from The Throne Room of God,
                emanate and dissipate across all the paths of man,
                emanate and flavour the taste buds of each favoured mouth,
                emanate and satisfy the styles and heeds of searching man.

The letterings of God within His missives are condensed and direct,
                              are counselling and true,

                        are facets of the truth needing to be directly
                              amplified and stressed,
                are essential and conducive to all
                              changes sought.

The letterings of God wake up the frostbitten and the snowflakes,
        wake up the iced up and the polar blasts,
        wake up the storm proof and the sun stricken,
        wake up the dried up and the waterproof.

The letterings of God address the aspects of man not receiving much attention,
        address the tried and true with wisdom to separate
                            the naïve and false,
        address the abilities of My sheep to adhere and understand,
        address the need to circulate and learn,
                to practise and assimilate,
                to acquire and respond,
                to dwell and overcome.

The letterings of God are not easily ignored unless foolishness is present,
                unless commitment is misplaced,
                unless the stars and stripes have completely
                          different meanings,
                unless shadow-boxing knows the imprints of
                          the devil.

The love and emphasis of God are on His encirclement of man,
        are on His restoration of man,
        are on His promises of The Cross,
        are on His sharing of an inheritance embedded in Eternity.

The love and emphasis of God fixate on benefitting man,
        fixate on accomplishing His Will,
        fixate on verifying The Freewill of man,
        fixate on honouring or respecting the freewill of man.

The love and emphasis of God are a love-fest born of sacrifice,
        are a love-fest born of His word,
        are a love-fest born of the promises for His Bride,
        are a love-fest born of His garden prepared for each child
                                    of God.

The love and emphasis of God are of agapé outreach,
        are for the companionable and loving,
        are for The Lambs and Sheep,
        are for all with an entry in The Lamb's Book of Life.

The eternal life with God reaches out for maturity on the third birthing—
                              from the grave of man.

Let those who can count to three know and understand.
Let those who cannot count to three both enquire and acquire.
Let those who teach,
>teach so The Lambs grow into Sheep.
Let those who think they are sheep not be acting like the goats."

My Content Study Aid

Introduction

These Divine letters mostly consist of Truth Statements intermixed with counselling and are presented for serious contemplation as to their ramifications and how we approach them in the conclusions we may draw. For they are filled with great significance for these present times.

I testify here to one and all that these letters are not of my writing nor instigation. These letters have all been dictated singularly, but in a cohesive grouping, by The Living God. They do not stand alone but smoothly build on the preceding ones as if designed as an unfolding story with an establishing foundation. Please take it, therefore, as a given as to the stated origin both by testimony and by claim.

The style of the book preserves the scribal comments in italics; while double quotation marks denote and enclose text of a divinely dictated origin. British spelling is used for reasons of national culture. Layout simplifies ease of reading and personal study. Each letter itself may be accurately searched from within His website. A concordance or a thesaurus has not been used at any stage prior to, during, or after the receiving of these texts. A dictionary, the Oxford Concise™, has sometimes been used to comprehend fully, the words of the divine voice used in expressing His intent. Because the letters have been received via dictation spoken by the divine voice directly into the mind, the punctuation is subject to human interpretation. Occasionally however, when required for clarity or emphasis, the capitalisation of words, together with the paragraphing, have also been indicated by The Divine. Minor spelling typos, with any other annoyances, are scribal; and the punctuation, together with the titles, usually are, but not always. Multiple subject matter sometimes occurs in a particular letter which precludes the naming of the letter being entirely appropriate with respect to descriptive accuracy.

Attached to the end of most items is My Content Study Aid inserted at the request of The Lord Jesus to enhance the benefits found in meditating on, and understanding, the hows and whys of the truth statements and His counselling as found herein. If no such study aid exists at the end of an item then there are additional journaling & notes pages provided in the appendix. Please remember this is your book to use in the way which best serves your growth within the discipleship of God.

Great care has been taken to ensure scribal accuracy in hearing and transcribing what are now these printed pages of divinely originated letters. Every word is as received without later omissions, additions, substitutions or edits.

May The Holy Spirit so testify as such to every enquiring soul.

Agapé,

Anthony,

His servant and His scribe.
Hamilton, New Zeland.

The Visiting of Megiddon

"The valley of Megiddon is soon to receive its visitors of purpose,
                its visitors chasing vengeance,
                its visitors seeking conflict:
                its visitors without remorse,
                    without mercy,
            without a worthwhile knowledge of The God of Israel.

The valley of Megiddon sits and waits,
            does nothing to hasten to its destiny,
            ignores the distant sounds of man,
            is quiescent in displaying the battlefield of God,
                    the battlefield of The Lord,
                    the battlefield of The Spirit's Fire,
                    the battlefield of the end-time of Israel.

The valley of Megiddon is peaceful in the sun,
            is a landscape which does not display the past,
                does not display the future,
            displays only the present in confirmation of a present time
                              of peace.

The valley of Megiddon with its plain of battle is a blood-soaked land,
                has been at the forefront of much hatred,
                      of much turmoil,
                      of much anger in despair.

The valley of Megiddon with its plain of battle has been an arena of the mournful,
            of the tears from wounded hearts,
            of the challenge to survive the daze of blows upon a head,
                  the daze of blood-loss to the soil,
                  the daze of loss of will when confronted by
                          the slaughter of the guilty,
                          the slaughter of the innocent,
                the slaughter where the dead remain uncounted
                          stretched out across the plain
                              in all the days of strife.

The days of strife are again unfolding in the heart of man,
                for man chooses to ignore the lessons available from history,
                    chooses to ignore the balance of the power,
                    chooses to ignore the feats available to his enemy of choice,
                    chooses to ignore the victory signs within the word of God,
                    chooses to ignore the certainty of defeat,
                    chooses to ignore the forecast of the outcome.

The days of strife are not many in number,
  are mostly spent in preparation,
    in garnishing the battlefield with fodder for
      the weapons,
    in selecting the bravest and the fittest to be the first
      to die,
  in selecting a place of safety from which to view the deeds of an assembled army,
    from which to view the coming deeds of God.

For as it is written so it will be deployed,
  so wrath will go to completion in My battle against the evil
    within man,
      which whispers in his ear,
      which contaminates his spirit,
      which captures his soul,
      which directs his freewill
        as if a robot running amok.

For as it is written so man encounters My Spirit's Fire to purify The Holy Land
  on which he stands,
  on which he rattles his sword in open defiance,
  on which he shouts his challenge to The God of Abraham,
  on which his legions have invaded on a quest for vengeance,
  on which,
    in foolishness,
      he calls The Risen Living God to account:
so The God of Israel mounts the rock and roars as
  The Mighty Lion of Judah surrounded by His Tribe."

My Content Study Aid

The Outreach of My People

"The outreach of My people is uncertain and spasmodic,
     is indifferent and random,
     is indefinite and chaotic.

The outreach of My people should tap a vein of gold,
     should avoid a prayer of rhetoric,
     should let My Spirit bring repentance to a soul.

The outreach of My people is to introduce,
     is to initiate a handshake,
     is to affirm the truth in testimony.

The outreach of My people is all about their testimonies of God,
     is all about their walk with God,
     is all about their discipling within the flock of God,
     is all about their commitment to their faith.

The outreach of My people is not inclusive of sharing a repetitious prayer:
       which has little impact on the heart of man,
       which is shed as easily as a shower on an oily coat,
       which is oft forgotten upon the setting of the sun.

The outreach of My people needs wisdom with understanding,
     needs My Spirit's Call,
     needs the opening of the heart with integrity of repentance,
     needs the heart-call of the age uttered by a soul in sorrow—
          with a new dawning in sight.

The outreach of My people is varied in approach,
     is varied in response,
     is varied according to the ability of My people—
          in hearing My Spirit's Call.

The outreach of My people should make use of The Word from God for the individual,
     should seek such in making their approach,
       in their daily appointments set by God,
    as the backbone of their outreach which testifies to each
         individual of being known by God.

 For this is the outreach of My people seen and heard in action,
         under the mantle of The Lord,
         in the preparing of My Spirit,
         in the sacrifice of The Father,
         in the offering of The Son.

 For this is the outreach of My people in which My Spirit moves,

in which testimonies are renewed,
are magnified,
are borne
are purposed to bring glory to
My name with salvation to the
seekers of the seed of faith.

For this is the outreach of My people:
to plant the seed of faith in fertile soil,
to ensure the tending of its growth,
to care for and protect the embryonic learning and discovery,
as a soul turns from its record of the past unto the promises
conveyed to man at Calvary—
as if splinters from The Cross—
as if unto the piercing and the cleaving
of the two-edged sword.

So the sword of My Spirit flashes in The Son-light,
separates—
disposes of—
the dross within a life of freewill without a gyroscope;
clears the way before—
placing new springs within the steps,
new vistas for the eyes,
new music for the ears,
new actions for the body,
new ways for the soul,
new guidance for the spirit:
new gifts poured out from within My Spirit's
charter for The Glory of My Temples.

So the outreach of My people extends the favour of God,
extends the outreach of the spirit,
soul and body,
extends a new option for a destiny—
a destiny with God.

So the outreach of My people extends the forecourt of each residence,
each courtyard of regality,
each court of holiness within the light.

So the outreach of My people extends the embellishments on The Gowns of Life,
extends the presence of The Throne Rooms,
extends relationships Born of Agapé Love."

The Decoration of The Heavens

"Behold!
    The stars are seated in the skies of The Son.
Behold!
    The suns of God are placed in the heavens of the sun of man.
Behold!
    The heavens of God are lit for display,
            are lit to aid discovery,
            are lit by way of proclamation,
            are lit so man may wonder,
            are lit so the steps of Man may know the steps of God,
            are lit so Man may seek his God—
    He who would have man come to dwell in his place prepared.
Behold!
    The scope of God stretched out by My hands.
Behold!
    The stretching written in My word long before man could comprehend,
               long before man learnt to measure,
    long before he had the power to tabulate The Edifice of God beyond The Earth.
Behold!
    The scope of God which does not shrink,
        which expands further to create,
        which reaches far beyond the counting ability of man,
            the naming ability of man,
            the visiting ability of man—
                while a mortal being of The Earth.
Behold!
    The scope of God in The Glory of His Firmament.
Behold!
    The imprint of The Lord subject to the imaging of man.
Behold!
    The lacework of eternity within the scope of man.
Behold!
    The future of the space-walk through the stars.
Behold!
    In anticipation,
        the visitations set for the eternity of man in the company of his God.
Behold!
    The wise who kneel in awe before the handiwork of God—

            the tableaux of The Master;
            the needlework of traceries;
            the engraving of designs of beauty;
            the intricacy of relationships;
      the setting of the motions both of dominance and servitude;
      the presentation of the seasons;
      the cycling of the heating and the cooling—
the resourcing of the needs of man on a lifeboat among the stars.

Behold!
    Man in his time of preparation for his eternal destiny.

Behold!
    Man in his wisdom and his folly.

Behold!
    Man suited to his immortality enthroned with grace.

Behold!
    Man restricted and dispossessed in the absence of mercy.

Behold!
    Man's journeying in gratitude.

Behold!
    Man's imprisonment in shame.

Behold!
    The childhood of man in the oversight of his God.

Behold!
    The being of man with accountability to his God for his freewill choice of destiny,
        seen here still playing with his toys,
        frittering away his time on trivia,
        leaving in effect that of fearful consequence,
        paying no regard to The Call of God.

Behold!
    The Son upon The Cross,
    the connecting of the laminin,
    the signposting of God among the stars.

Behold!
    The gifts of My Spirit;
    the tongues of Heaven;
    the testimonies of answered prayer;
    the capabilities of the molecules in the cells of life;
    the reality of God within the lives of My people:
    the whereabouts of My thumbprint left fully on display.

Behold!
    Are they seen yet without understanding?

Are they encountered yet dismissed?

Are they experienced yet without belief as truth?

Behold!
> The questioning of man by God,
>> with requirement for the answers,
>>> which records responses for the day of accounting,
>>> which is ignored at man's peril of the second death.

Behold!
> The vibrancy of God would have man enlist as His companion in His fellowship of the stars."

My Content Study Aid

The Wastelands of God

"The wastelands of God are the dead zones of creation,
        of where there is no life,
        of where existence is limited to God,
        of where the needs of life are yet to be accumulated,
        of where the location has the parameters for life still unset by God,
        of where the nursery for creation is running wild and unfurnished,
        of where the zoning is unfriendly to the life envisaged,
        of where the new beginning is still awaiting
                the creation of the birthplace,
                the creation of protection,
                the creation of the species in accord with His Will.

The creation of a species requires the assembling of the building blocks,
        the tweaking of the strain control,
        the adjustments for the senses,
        the bestowing of the means of movement within the planned environment,
        the selecting of appearance,
        the placement of the appendages;
        establishing an interlocking chain of food,
        setting the effort for predation,
        modifying the skin for function,
        fixing the rate of metabolism,
        attending to the steps within digestion,
        choosing from a multitude of reflex actions—
                through the synapses of an in-line circuitry—
                to the remoteness of a brain,
        determining the circulation of the nutrients,
        installing the armour—
                or protection—
        for the day or night as generated.

The creation of a species requires originality,
                is the concept of integration on a scale of grand design—
                      so non-intended conflicts are avoided both in time and space,
                      so each species has access to success according to intent:
                              while free from incidents threatening longevity of being.

The creation of a species must address its preservation,
                anticipate a gradual adaptation with its breeding line secure,
                      while prolificacy is related as a subset of reproduction.

The creation of a species has no role for chance,
        is established on the principles of life from the blocks controlling compilation

of the code:
structured so to handle the needs of updating,
over-riding,
duplication,
together with variance of the individual and continuation for the generations—
in a storehouse of efficiency.

The storehouse of efficiency needs to be memory dependent,
memory maintaining,
memory correcting,
memory serving,
memory recording,
memory deleting:
with a controller resident in the storehouse which can call the tune;
which can read the breathing of new life into an inert shell;
which can control all aspects of an entity of being—
throughout the repetitions of the cycle of life.

The wastelands of God are visited by God,
are at the direction of God,
exist because of God,
change through the objective of God,
settle in perfection within The Will of God.

The wastelands of God become the fertile and the productive,
the washed and the refreshed,
the carpeted and the homelands;
are surveyed by God and pronounced as good and bountiful,
as the homelands now take due prominence in the sight of God.

The wastelands of God are never without promise,
are never without commitment to finality,
are never described correctly when tied to the land descriptive,
are from the outset endowed with destinies of composition
as systems born for supporting life:
of systems in the making yet presently hostile to the life each is targeted to carry,
of systems composing within the mists,
composing within the vapours,
composing within the liquids,
composing within the dust,
composing within the clouds,
composing within The Mind of God—
of systems being set upon a roadway to success.

For as each is instilled by God,
so it is enabled to bear."

The Inside of The Eyelids

"The inside of the eyelids of man are the screens of scenes,
        are the screens fitted for reception of projection,
        are the screens fitted for communication,
        are the screens fitted for Sighted Telepathy with God.

The inside of the eyelids are sensitive and definitive,
        are secured and private,
        are for the holy and the sacred,
        are for the revealing of the intent of God.

The inside of the eyelids have almost closed positions,
        work in unison together,
        have colour at the switch,
        can be focussed on with intent,
        can change the direction of the motion,
        can determine the centre of display.

The inside of the eyelids are tuned for display,
        require waiting on The Lord,
        are prepared for access,
        have beauty within their bounds,
        intimate the things of God to The Servants of The Lord.

The inside of the eyelids are the screens of God,
        are fragile in displays as for the stopping of transmission,
        are for when in a place of uninterrupted rest,
        are managed by My Spirit,
        are for those who converse with God,
                who know His voice,
                who know His tongues with understanding,
                who can both receive and impart the things of God:
                        within The Tasking of His Servant.

The inside of the eyelids are not there to imprison man in darkness,
        to just safeguard the eyes,
        to leave him groping for his way,
        to leave him in need of a guiding hand,
        to leave him as the blind and blinded:
                without a testimony of healing.

The inside of the eyelids are there to portray the light of Christ,
        to bring the magnificence of creation as reality,
        to call My servants past the stumbling blocks,
                past the times of faltering,

> past the attacks of demons,
> past sojourning in a wilderness:
> into the presence of The Lord.

The inside of the eyelids serve My servants when in isolation,
> when removed against their will,
> when companionship is limited,
> when input to the spirit is restricted by man.

The inside of the eyelids are of benefit when counsel is being sought,
> when the way of progress is unclear,
> when man in need of prayer is scheduled to present before My servant,
> when confirmation of the truth is being sought.

The inside of the eyelids are fitted to bring sound,
> are fitted to convey the understanding as required by God,
> are fitted with the visual and the audio—
> the links enabled for the reception of the telepathic transmissions from The Lord.

The inside of the eyelids grow and develop with the practise of My disciples,
> with the use employed,
> with the experience gained:
> for as a toddler learns to walk,
> so the eyelid turns from being a shutter bringing darkness to a curtain disclosing light."

My Content Study Aid

_____
_____
_____
_____
_____
_____
_____
_____
_____
_____
_____
_____
_____
_____
_____

Veins and Arteries

"The veins of My church have been in use for the centuries of man,
        have sometimes shrunk and shrivelled,
        have sometimes burst forth into blossom with the promise of the harvest,
        have oft-times fed and watered with very little movement.

The veins of My church should stand out and expand,
        should be very easily followed to the heart,
        should feed all from the outskirts into the centre of activity.

The veins of My church should sometimes split and concentrate,
        should create a well for the birthing of the future stars,
        should dip in for the nourishment without the fear of starving.

The veins of My church are long reaching with the pathways clearly marked,
        gather in the clusters,
        reach up to the heavens,
        discover circulation.

The veins of My church can be hidden out of sight,
        can be enlarged from the workload of the day,
        can be bypassed for another,
        can feel the pain of substitution which does not acknowledge love.

The veins of My church can feel the touch of frost which withers the tender tips,
        which leaves them unattached,
        which knows the sounds of discord growing louder as they feed.

The veins of My church breathe and navigate,
        circulate and articulate,
        pulse and vibrate with the life within.

The veins of My church are nourished by the new additions to the streams,
        the immersions in the streams,
        the supping from the streams,
        the blessings and the nourishment carried by
                the streams—
    the streams destined to enhance the river as the artery of new life
        spreading across the homelands of the saints.

The arteries of God carry good news to distant shores,
        to distant homes,
        to distant lives.

The arteries of God are replenished and renewed,
        are refreshed and refurbished,
        are resplendent and responsive:

> as they penetrate the areas where faith is at a premium,
> as they relax and recuperate where faith is quite at home.

The arteries of God reveal afresh the activities of God,
> turn up the heat for souls and spirits slumbering to keep warm,
> bring comfort with encouragement to where duress has laid its head,
> call the labourers to hasten with the crop before the storms arrive;
> select the servants for the messaging of God,
> oversee the saints in their maturity as they protect the visions
>> which are known:
> to drive the arteries with direction into their destinations.

So the dreams of man become the reality of God.
So the faceprint lying in the dirt becomes the visage known to angels.
So the testing of a heart of shame becomes the mindset of the valiant of endeavour.
So the least of man becomes The Elect of God."

***Scribal Note*:** Refer to: 'Prayers within Eternity', Bk7 *GOD Speaks to His Edifice*.

My Content Study Aid

_____
_____
_____
_____
_____
_____
_____
_____
_____
_____
_____
_____
_____
_____
_____
_____
_____
_____
_____

The Waterways of God

"The waterways of God flow outward in one direction,
      flow according to the spirit,
      flow according to the soul of domination.

The waterways of God seek the shortest course,
      can get hung up in a pond while waiting for the overflow.

The waterways of God can mark the sources,
      can mark the courses,
      can mark the length of flow,
      can mark the rate of flow,
      can end up in the bathmats for the eyes.

The waterways of God are the release points as at the spillways of a dam,
      the spillways filling each tail-race with emotions running raw,
            with uncapped feelings,
            with distant memories,
            with intense disappointment,
            with inexpressible joy:
         when the words of the soul are overtaken,
            are exhausted,
            become inadequate;
      with the surfacing of the spirit at a needed point in time.

The waterways of God can have a sound all of their own,
      need no query as to their origin,
      are identified with ease.

The waterways of God are reserved for the intellect of man as the alarm bells of the spirit:
      as the bells of loneliness,
      as the bells of celebration;
      as the bells of frustration,
      as the bells of bitterness released;
      as the bells warning of nearby hidden rocks,
      as the bells within a lighthouse on a foggy night.

The waterways of God often carry sounds without the wetting,
      speak of the young in need,
      are the call-outs for some mothering,
      are the requests for loving arms.

The waterways of God speak a language all their own,
      speak a language showing need of consolation,
         showing need of urgency,
         showing need of companionship,

                    showing need of comforting:
                            as the spirit cries.

The spirit cries with reason:
        cries for attention,
        cries in despair,
        cries in mourning for the loved,
        cries in desperation for the lost.

The spirit cries at the depression of the soul,
        at the marks of Cain,
        at a marriage degenerating into violence,
        at a vision received which can no longer be fulfilled,
        at betrayal of a contract no longer held as sacred.

The waterways of God shed and recover,
        water and stain,
        dry-up and restore.

The waterways of God dissipate the surplus which breaks restraint,
        the surplus built upon injustice,
        the surplus built upon elation:
        the surplus which brings the soundings of the spirit,
and so provides a record either for a bench or for an entry:
                against a record within The Book of Life."

My Content Study Aid

The Vagrancy of The Youth

"The vagrancy of the youth speaks of a further generation becoming lost to God,
                becoming lost to their parents' order,
                becoming lost to all authority—
                            both guiding and directing.

The vagrancy of the youth speaks of lack of drive,
                of motivation,
                of a standard in their lives.

The vagrancy of the youth has toes that kick the dust,
                has the daring of their peers,
                has little self-control when gathered in a group,
                has no respect for others with all which that implies.

The vagrancy of the youth knows the effects of alcohol guzzled in excess,
                knows the beat of rhythms where the words reflect their lives,
                  where the risk of abandonment rises with the time,
                    where the speech does not enhance a standing before the
                                            God who hears.

The vagrancy of the youth is shallow in responsibility,
                is the products of their parents,
                is accustomed to curse and swear,
                is loose in their behaviour,
                is not encouraged in the home,
                is half-hearted in the effort to fend off the distasteful
                                                and the wayward.

The vagrancy of the youth builds to the iniquity of man;
the discord of the youth leads to the homeless and the careless;
the slyness of the youth brings disparagement—
                              with despoilment to the fore.

The vagrancy of the youth brings machinations before the courts,
                speaks of stupidity in action,
                brings curfews down on heads,
                starts the cars without the keys,
                lives the chase without concern,
                brings disasters on the heels of rebels without a cause.

The vagrancy of the youth can shatter and destroy the hopes of generations,
                can violate a promise as easily as the breaking of a bottle,
                can resort to violence in the taking of possession,
                can dictate with a swagger and a leer upon a face,
                can rush to hide in an instant at the turning of the tables,

can resort to bringing harm when freedom is impaired.

The vagrancy of the youth circulates in a culture without caring;
        ripens for entrance to a gang,
        practises in their youth for adeptness in maturity.

The vagrancy of the youth trains ability to take, does not
        teach of giving, restricts the
        attitude of sharing.

The vagrancy of the youth is a pipeline to the extremes of selfishness,
        expounds on I see I want I take,
            may be a passing phase when rescue is attempted,
            may be the precursor to a life filled with correction.

Beware the vain and the proud:
        for theirs is a lonely walk.

Beware those still uneducated for mixing in society:
        for theirs meets frustration head on with a lack of words,
            with a lack of understanding,
            with a lack of writing and of skills.

Beware the poor in spirit where most is out of reach.

Beware the soul despairing which manifests in anger.

Beware the storms which gather with the recruits prepared.

Beware the vagrant youth of man where respect is not instilled,
        where the night is as a playground for the soul,
        where freewill is built on the mischief of success.

The vagrancy of the youth meets with a turning point in life on encountering
                The God of love."

My Content Study Aid

_____

_____

_____

_____

_____

_____

_____

_____

_____

The Vacuum of Space

"The vacuum of space is not really so,
        depends upon the sophistication of the measurements,
        depends upon location,
        depends upon the perspective,
        depends upon the mass deciding the extent of gravity.

The vacuum of space depends upon the definition implicit in the understanding—
    the compendium of composition comprising that with referral named as space,
    the degree of lack of the quantity of energy expected to be absent in a vacuum,
        expected not to reside as mass,
        expected to not be as atmospheres within the bounds of gravity.

For the vacuum of space has light traversing on its journeys,
    has waves which are difficult to verify,
    has the chattering of the stars on wavelengths far above the present audio of man,
    has collisions in the making as masses come and go,
    has the particles of sunlight streaming gases from afar,
    has the dusts of aeons circling in their rings.

For the vacuum of space is a very busy place:
        has travellers leaving trails,
        has travellers making waves,
        has travellers with protection from intrusion,
        has travellers with no thought of right-of-way,
        has travellers who cannot stop if a warning flashes red,
        has travellers who have been trapped for a very long long time,
        has travellers without the companionship of life.

For the vacuum of space stretches past the imaginings of man,
        tests his comprehension of one with many zeros—
    where commas do not help the cause,
    where the faster travellers still grow weak and dim,
    where the distant past discloses what may no longer be,
    where man may never travel unless dressed in the gown of God.

So the gown of God dresses man for eternity,
        makes the present impossibility into the practicality of the presently,
        converts by scale reduction all the distant sites,
                hidden by the zeros,
            into the presence known to God.

So the gown of God becomes the dressing of the chrysalis of man—
                upon emergence from the grave.
So the gown of God becomes a symbol of perfection,

the enabling of the spirit and the soul,
the touchstone of the heavens which then knows the fall of fire:
    upon the gold of purity,
        the gold without contamination,
        the gold which has passed through The Refiner's Fire unto reward."

My Content Study Aid

The Viceroy of India

"The Viceroy of India spoke with authority in the past,
                in an office of Viceroyalty,
                from territory so governed for a distant king.

The Viceroy of India spoke upon a field of grandeur,
                upon a field of disparities,
                upon a field born of a distant past.

The Viceroy of India spoke according to the options,
                according to instructions,
                according to the policy of the day.

The Viceroy of India sought to preserve the rule of law,
                sought transitioning in peace,
                sought consensus among conspirators,
                sought wisdom among dissent.

The Viceroy of India asked the impossible
                      from those engaged in self-interest of minorities,
                      from those engaged in fragmentation of the whole,
                      from those engaged in creating homelands for the few,
                      from those engaged in birthing new divisions.

The Viceroy of India was presiding at the closing of an epoch,
            had the visionless clawing so to feed,
            had the gods of idolatry shouting in discord,
            had the bounds of law dismembering as he spoke.

The Viceroy of India was presiding over an office due for extinction,
       an office no longer able to gather resources to protect the imperilled and at risk,
       an office where the seal of the king was already gathering dust—
                                from an ink pad which was dry.

The Viceroy of India saw the sun set very quickly,
                saw the slaughter of the helpless in the names of unloving gods,
                saw the tears of anguish on the face of many,
                saw the time to go had come:
        and left amidst the turmoil as differences were settled by the sword.

The Viceroy of India had a godly disposition but was overcome by the intensity of evil,
                as the vision vanished,
                as the picture changed,
                as his forces ran away,
                as mayhem presided within the losing of control.

As The Son returns to receive His kingdom,

so the potentates will likewise fall,
so their authority will flee with the expanse of freedom,
so the collapse of the tenures of the kings of The Earth—
        whether elected or inherited or assumed—
will accompany the mouths of evil,
    the sinning against God,
        the battles of My Spirit in the land of Goshen.

As The Son returns so My Bride is readied,
    so My Bride is entailed,
    so My Bride receives as co-heirs of the kingdom's reign.

As The Son returns so evil is attenuated,
    so justice is to the fore,
    so My Banner heralds,
        marks,
        proclaims and flies.

So The Kings of Salem walk up to their thrones.

So the worshipful of God exchange their faith for wisdom.

So the wise are instated and deemed as fit to rule in righteousness.

As The Son is seated,
    so The Father blesses;
    so The Spirit speaks unto the assembly gathered;
    so The Gowns of Life testify to the viceroys of the present,
        enhancing their surroundings.

My Content Study Aid

The Disappointments of God

"Scattered is the flock of God upon The Earth.

Widespread is the acceptance of The Saviour within The Field of Grace.

Impressive is the reaching to the stars of The Edifice of God on Earth.

Disappointing is the standard of morality within My church,
                              within My pastorates,
                              within My elderships,
                              within the flock all claiming to be sheep.

Disappointing is the mocking of My Word,
                the twisting of The Meaning,
                the taking Out of Context,
                the ending of a sentence at A Comma,
                the seeking of alternatives to interpolations which may best convey:
                              the interpretation of the meaning wanting Confirmation.

Disappointing are the ways of scholars claiming to be learned,
                              yet failing the test of a relationship with God,
                              yet failing the perceiving of The Word of God,
                              yet failing the commissioning of God.

Disappointing is the mediocrity of prayer—
                as measured by its length,
                as equated to the sincerity of the heart,
                as gauged by its coverage when posing as if diarrhoea of the mouth.

Disappointing is the extent of the clamour of the soul within the spirit's bounds of
                                                a damaged temple—
                far from upright,
                far from righteous,
                far from its spirit's standard for the safe keeping of the soul.

Disappointing is the paucity of the witnessing of My Blood,
                              the testifying of The Sacrifice of The Son—
                                            among the saints across The Earth:
                              as deployed with Grace for an offered destiny to the lost.

Disappointing is the end-time tribulation as it falls on those who think they are immune,
                        as they clutch a covenant in tatters,
                        as they mouth the prayers which cascade to the floor,
                        as they attribute that to which they are not entitled,
                        as they impart damnation to their souls.

I,
    The Lord,

say to all those this day,
> 'Uplift Instate Instill.
>
> Repent Renew Restore.'

For such as these should attend,
> be taught and learn the active ways of God without delay.

For such as these lead a life of self-deception,
> dwell in the land of make-believe,
> ignore the application of My word well preached—
> > to their lives still living in denial of wise counsel.

For such as these are blind to miracles allowed no impact on a memory,
> permitted no effect upon a life,
> sequestered in the trash can with no promise of release.

The disappointments of God record the spurning of grace,
> record repentance undeclared,
> record the casualness of the soul,
> record the issues of morality,
> record the lack of testimony,
> record the covenant no longer held as holy,
> record the absence of the fear of God.

The building of a shameful record may be measured,
> may be assessed,
> may qualify for the end-time receiving of My wrath.

The building of a shameful record does not pre-empt erasure of the slate—
> upon the heart's sincerity of the request for grace.

For grace in action is a wonder to behold,
> with a marvel in the making.

Behold the miracle of forgiveness with the changes wrought within a soul."

My Content Study Aid

_____
_____
_____
_____
_____
_____

The Clavicles of Grace

"The clavicles of grace are the coat hangers of the gowns of God,
of The Gowns of Life,
of the gowns befitting purity both of thought and of surroundings.

The clavicles of grace are the architecture for the new body of man as founded
for eternity.

The clavicles of grace resize and stretch,
compress and squeeze,
enlarge and expand,
always fit each gown of inheritance,
always permit free passage,
always permit freedom of movement,
always impel at the speed of thought.

The clavicles of grace conform with the intellect of man.

The clavicles of grace confer the ability to change,
the ability to process,
the ability to enact the senses,
the ability to navigate dimensions,
the ability to share,
the ability to exhibit multi-presence,
the ability to dwell within the heavens and the presence of God.

The clavicles of grace do not need recharging,
ride the rails of energy undefiled by use,
can travel faster than movement can be realised,
can decode the messaging of the surroundings as directed with specifics.

The clavicles of grace know the expressways and the byways,
know the locations deemed inestimable by God,
know the masterpieces installed for man to visit,
know the clavicles of linkage arising from mortality,
know the clavicles of beings as they comprise the hosts.

The clavicles of grace know the clavicles of God within The Family of God.

The clavicles of grace oscillate at frequencies beyond man's present understanding,
can fit them to the current dimensions of enclosure,
know the means of entry,
know all the books within the library,
understand the data trails,
comprehend the riding of the pathway formed from the homing beams of light.

The clavicles of grace have multi-access to communications,

        have multi-media readily available,
        have recordings ready for replaying,
        have memories at instant recall.

The clavicles of grace offer access to the music of the heavens,
        to the choirs of angels,
        to the singing with one accord,
        to the wisdom of the ages built upon the envelopes of man,
        to the wisdom of God built upon His eternal love."

My Content Study Aid

The Land of Goshen

"The fortitude of the saints must not waver under trial,
                must not submit to the hounds of terror,
                must not flee from the dragon's breath.

The fortitude of the saints must strengthen and sustain,
                must support and uphold,
                must respond and skirmish.

The fortitude of the saints must not dwell within a rest home:
                must be healthy and vibrant,
                must be eager and enthusiastic,
                must be pronounced and proclaimed.

The fortitude of the saints must not become inept,
                must not become replaced by frailty,
                must not become the will of yesterday.

The fortitude of the saints is required to see survival,
                is required to escape the foe,
                is required to repair the armour damaged in a battle
                                      in the land of Goshen.

The land of Goshen is a land at risk,
            is a land subject to the eyes of envy,
            is a land where peace exists,
            is a land where weapons have been turned to ploughshares,
            is a land where families are nurturing their young,
                where the defences are not great,
                where neighbours are quite distant,
                where protection is the sea which lies within the power of God.

The land of Goshen is the land where the land is tilled,
                where the land grows grass,
                where the land is stocked,
                where the land from afar appears to be there for the taking.

The land of Goshen is the land of milk and honey,
            is the land of smiles and welcomes,
            is the land which countenances the handshake born of greeting—
                                and a close-up view of eyes.

The land of Goshen is a land of future wealth;
            is a land blessed with the warming of the waters,
                with the filling of the granaries,
                with the overflowing of the wine skins,
                with the presence of The God of Grace.

The land of Goshen fills the cargo ships with produce for distant trades,
                has governors who govern,
                has scribes aplenty in the multitude,
                has stability in the home land,
                has been and is surveyed by opportunists awaiting a chance to seize.

The land of Goshen has spoils awaiting exhumation,
                awaiting exploitation,
                awaiting delivery to willing markets.

The land of Goshen is a prize worth plucking:
                for resources buried deep below,
                for resources in the distance yet to be unearthed,
                for resources in the depths which can both feed and grow.

The land of Goshen is seen as well worth harvesting,
                is seen as a place worth capturing,
                is seen as both prolific and unprotected,
                is seen as worth the risk of brazen seizure with a display of force.

The land of Goshen is in need of allies of renown,
    of allies without threats,
    of allies with honest records,
    of allies who are not self-serving,
    of allies without encumbrances,
    of allies of just cause,
    of allies who do not circumvent the law,
    of allies with integrity of purpose,
    of allies who know the strength in numbers,
    of allies who are the masters of opinion,
    of allies who can differentiate between the rights and wrongs,
    of allies who have not forsaken the golden rule of justice,
    of allies who seek partnerships of honour,
    of allies who do not visit in the night,
    of allies who do not fleece and cheat,
        who do not confess to jealousy yet know it very well,
        who do not look across the fence then try to move the boundary,
    of allies who will not pack and leave with the gathering of the storm clouds,
    of allies who know what it is like to be cast aside as victims,
    of allies who know what it is like to encounter frost as pressure is applied.

So it is God awaits a call for friendship,
                awaits a call of reciprocating love,
                awaits a call which moves an anthem in its fullness up onto the stage
                                                          of life—
            for the world at large to see and hear and read.

    For as the testimony is borne so will My Spirit move."

"Let the Land of Goshen declare its National Anthem."

Scribal Note: *This may be found at the following link:*
https://www.thewebsiteofthelord.org.nz/Resources/NZ+National+Anthem++Flag.html
*and click on the Video Clip: Bill Johnson's Thoughts on The NZ National Anthem
as Published by Keith Wagener (Used by Permission)*

The National Anthem of New Zealand

God Defend New Zealand

God of nations! at Thy feet
In the bonds of love we meet,
Hear our voices, we entreat,
God defend our Free Land.
Guard Pacific's triple star,
From the shafts of strife and war,
Make her praises heard afar,
God defend New Zealand.

Men of ev'ry creed and race
Gather here before Thy face,
Asking Thee to bless this place,
God defend our Free Land.
From dissension, envy, hate,
And corruption guard our State,
Make our country good and great,
God defend New Zealand.

Peace, not war, shall be our boast,
But, should foes assail our coast,
Make us then a mighty host,
God defend our Free Land.
Lord of battles in thy might,
Put our enemies to flight,
Let our cause be just and right,
God defend New Zealand.

Let our love for Thee increase,
May Thy blessings never cease,
Give us plenty, give us peace,
God defend our Free Land.
From dishonour and from shame
Guard our country's spotless name
Crown her with immortal fame,
God defend New Zealand.

May our mountains ever be
Freedom's ramparts on the sea,
Make us faithful unto Thee,
God defend our Free Land.
Guide her in the nations' van,
Preaching love and truth to man,
Working out Thy Glorious plan,
God defend New Zealand.

The Eternity of God

"The eternity of God is not an existence filled with the dilemma of idleness,
       is not an existence filled with searching for the reason to justify the being,
       is not an existence built upon surroundings remaining static,
       is not an existence where jobs are allocated out upon request,
       is not an existence commensurate with the mortality of man,
       is not an existence where boredom is the enemy of man.

The eternity of God is filled with the storytelling of creation:
          with the participation of creation,
          with the recreation of creation,
          with the learning of creation,
          with the responsibility of creation,
          with the justice of creation,
          with the life-blood of creation,
          with the rectitude of creation.

The eternity of God is the backdrop for the garden party of creation,
          both of the presence greeted and of the absence noted.

The eternity of God is consistent with the information tendered,
              does not vary with time,
     is the home of concepts unknown to mortal man,
     is the future within the past,
     is the past within the future,
     is both within the present.

The eternity of God can run time as it pleases,
     can still time as it pleases,
     can have a viewpoint dependent on a declaration
              as to the start and end,
              as to the continuation of the present,
              as to the continuation being absent.

The eternity of God is filled with great joy and endeavour,
        with great celebrations and achievements,
        with great movements and appearances.

The eternity of God is filled with all the things of God,
        with all the beings of God,
        with all the settings of God.

The eternity of God is filled with all the imaginings of God readied for disclosure unto
                              the face of all who love Him.

The eternity of God is as a supermarket without end:

where every aisle is filled with new visions worth investigation,
with new relationships to birth,
with new protocols to learn,
where the footnotes to the stars can be amended by a visit,
can be moved by a word,
can be enthroned for life,
can be instances of freewill—
yet capable of exhibiting great purity when mediated by God."

My Content Study Aid

The Camaraderie of The Soul

"The camaraderie of the soul inhibits and exhibits when withdrawn from the spirit.

The camaraderie of the soul is easily inducted into the hall of infamy,
                      is difficult to polish for to shine in the hall of fame.

The camaraderie of the soul adjusts to its surroundings on starting a new beginning—
                  whether at the tipping point of a dusk or of a dawn.

The camaraderie of the soul needs training in its preferences for the selections to be
                                              instilled if it:
                      is to find its way to majesty;
                      is to forsake the darkness it knows so well.

The camaraderie of the soul is a strange acquaintance of the spirit,
        for it can bite and snap,
            it can holler,
                scream and shout,
        it can be quiescent while the spirit is rejoicing,
        it can be blackened in its speech when in a swirling cesspit,
        it can be purified in essence when the spirit reigns.

The camaraderie of the soul can embarrass both the spirit and the body,
        can shame both the spirit and the body,
        can disgrace in waiting both the spirit and the body as they seek to recover
                              from the wounding of a wounded soul.

The camaraderie of the soul needs assistance with learning how to trust,
                with learning whom to trust,
                      with acquiring knowledge of the flavour of the truth.

The camaraderie of the soul needs forbearance as it attempts to climb where it may not
                                          have been before,
                where the feet are uncertain of their placement,
                where the hands are uncertain of the grip,
                where the mouth can hurl obscenities in the shadows and blessings
                                              in the sunlight.

The camaraderie of the soul should not be over-polished so it sees the image known
                                                        from yesterday,
                rather should it focus on the clarity of the vision as reflected:
                that which can be enlarged into the morrow with the steps into
                                  eternity and the handclasp of God.

The camaraderie of the soul seeks guidance as it clears its decks of clutter,
                      as it clear s the holds of lies,
                      as it clears the smoke stack of its smoke,

as it clears the portholes of the hiding knaves,
as it polishes the engine room for new voyages of discovery,
as it clears and purges all in preparation with a new captain
at the helm.

The camaraderie of the soul sails a certain sea when fitted with a compass which is true,
with a captain who knows the harbour at the journey's end:
with all the inbound hidden rocks,
with all the whirlpools and the whirlwinds,
with all that which would impale a soul and parade its very being.

The camaraderie of the soul may need a change of crew,
together with the stripping of the barnacles,
so the intended anchorage may be safe and sure and the voyage not delayed
along the way.

So the greeting of the spirit and the body may bring unity of purpose inclusive
of the soul."

My Content Study Aid

_____
_____
_____
_____
_____
_____
_____
_____
_____
_____
_____
_____
_____
_____
_____
_____
_____
_____
_____
_____

The Faith of Man

"The gradient of life gets steeper with ascent.

The gradient of life becomes more even with a crowd.

The gradient of life widens as it flattens with descent.

The gradient of life measures the development of life,
        measures the intensity of life,
        measures the level of intelligence,
            the becoming self-aware,
            the active use of weapons,
            the expression of emotions,
            the seeking of comfort for an injury,
            the acknowledging of counsel,
            the social order as achieved,
            the means of reproduction,
            the method of dispersion,
            the time spent by the young in immaturity.

The gradient of life has man lifted up and out of reach,
        has man fallen and left for dead,
        records the conflicts found in status,
            the conflicts in procurement,
            the conflicts of consumption,
            the conflicts present in accumulating gain,
                      in achievement in the face of least effort,
                      in wealth not seen as out of reach.

The gradient of life is influenced by the gradient of games,
            by the gradient of homes,
            by the gradient of livelihoods,
            by the gradient of education of the young,
            by the gradient of modes of travel,
            by the gradient of selection as a spouse,
            by the gradient of the welfare of a family,
            by the gradient of commitment to a covenant.

The gradient of life has the gradient of evil embedded,
        awaits the grafting in of the gradient of righteousness enamoured of freewill.

The gradient of evil fills the headlines with despair,
                with infamy,
                with fortunes of the cursed.

The gradient of righteousness is without slope,
            is a straight and level line throughout existence,

> is pre-empted for the headline space,
> is content with a byline in the eaves,
> appears when evil is absent from the voice deserving of the attention of man.

The gradient of righteousness is drawn when Righteous Faith is conspicuously installed
> within the spirit and the soul.

Faith holds its ground before the blows of evil un-contained.

Faith is dragged into the mire by the dirges of the evil;
Faith is shrugged off by the passers-by;
Faith is not acknowledged by the sinful with intent.

Faith evaporates when faced with the ravages of man;
Faith weakens on viewing the battlefields of man;
Faith expires where encouragement is absent;
Faith deserts when attracted by understanding;
Faith cries out for comfort when sequestered;
Faith becomes unknown when generations do not hear a testimony.

Faith dissipates in the absence of the blood;
Faith is insulated when communication fails;
Faith wanders to and fro when the way is lost.

Faith lies unrewarded when the race lies uncompleted;
Faith is not on lips when it is most needed.

Faith is surrendered by a willing heart;
Faith is usurped upon consent.

Faith is built upon The Headlines of Good News.

Faith arises upon stirring;
Faith commits on proclamation;
Faith consumes on receiving of The Fire;
Faith builds on immediacy of the answer;
Faith increases with the sound of thunder.

Faith is magnified by The Reading of The Word;
Faith is upheld by two or three together;
Faith is unbridled as The White Horse Rider searches for The Arrows;
Faith is set free when The Lion of Judah roars;
Faith is acclaimed in the presence of The Spirit;
Faith is sought when the road is filled with rocks;
Faith is enhanced on stories of success.

Faith grows by leaps and bounds with The Witnessing of Miracles;
Faith is there in excess at Divine Appointments;
Faith grows with Healing Answered Prayer;
Faith achieves great victories in The Lands of Idols;

Faith magnifies where Abilities cannot Aid;
Faith supplies When Asked.

Faith increases with a need;
Faith overcomes when met with confrontation;
Faith hears The Tongues of Heaven instructing the spirit and the soul;
Faith envelops as Love Conquers All;
Faith stands straight before the downtrodden;
Faith is upright beside those calling for support.

Faith is beckoned as the gifts are deployed;
Faith beckons as the gifts are employed;
Faith confirms as angels form a circle;
Faith is present in each Temple of The Spirit;
Faith supports an answer to a need made known.

Faith holds dear The Promises of God.

Faith attends The Spoken Word of God,
    presents in righteousness,
    upholds in holiness,
    blossoms with each spirit in communication with his God:
                    for the welfare of each soul.

Faith is going to arise from The Trials of man,
        from The End-time Need for Faith,
        from The Encouragement of God."

My Content Study Aid

The Welcome of The Centuries

"The welcome of the centuries awaits man in faith upon the sounding of The Trumpet.

The welcome of the centuries speaks of much preparation,
        speaks of every thing in place,
        speaks of sin relegated to the outfield—
                far from any influence on The Field of Glory.

The welcome of the centuries sees The Fruit of Faith rewarded within a scene of blessing,
        within a scene of great significance,
        within a scene besetting a sea change on The Earth.

The welcome of the centuries removes the mat from before an opened doorway
                for The Stars,
        removes the hindrance of uncertainty which has bedevilled the past,
        removes the word bound in a promise into the reality of the present.

The welcome of the centuries places The King among the kings,
        The Shepherd with His flock,
        The Lion of Judah with His pride,
        The Son with His co-heirs of inheritance,
        The Father with His family of greeting in adoption,
        The Holy Spirit with His torchlight raised high
                before His graduands of discipleship,
        The Lord Jesus with His Bride affirmed with
                      full rejoicing.

The welcome of the centuries witnesses a departure with a greeting,
        verifies the healthiness of the soul,
        testifies of the leading of the spirit of man
                and completion of the task.

The welcome of the centuries witnesses the soul receiving the handshake of eternity,
        acknowledges a relationship established unto completion,
        testifies of the unity of the soul and the spirit
                in perfect harmony.

The welcome of the centuries witnesses the fulfilment of The Promises of God,
        bequeaths endowments becoming due,
        testifies of the successful calling of The Bride unto the presence of her
                King.

The welcome of the centuries reverses an earlier departure
                within the annals of the ministry of man,
                within the annals of the registry of God,
    within the annals held in faith as bestowed on every generation with knowledge

of The New Covenant as declared.

The welcome of the centuries is extended to the faithful and the fearful—
                    the watchers and the waiters—
                    the sheep and the lambs:
           those who have each shed their heart of sin,
                     have each presented with their temple,
                     have each received their gown of life.

For such as they are The Victors of a Race well run,
           with greetings as they finish upon the making of a call,
           with selection of the destiny confirmed by the outcomes
                     inherent in every freewill choice.

For such as they are The Children of God—
           The Sons and Daughters of The Living God.

For such as they are The Stars of God.

For such as they are those on whom His Glory Falls,
           on whom His Glory Builds,
           on whom His Glory Extends the welcome of the centuries."

My Content Study Aid

_____
_____
_____
_____
_____
_____
_____
_____
_____
_____
_____
_____
_____
_____
_____
_____
_____
_____

The Means of Man

"The stepping stones across the fording of a river,
  the stepladder reaching to the highest branches,
  the staircase leading from the floor below to all the floors above:
      such as these are designed to transport safely,
          have no shortcuts built in for the nimble,
          have no shortcuts for the tired,
          have no shortcuts to achieving of a goal.

  For each has its peculiarities that speaks to the spirit and the soul.

The stepping stones require certainty of placement of each foot in a sequence—
                which is obvious,
     will not allow completion of a dry shod journey
        if usage is without due concentration:
        if one is bypassed in a hurry,
        if one is dwelling underwater and cannot fulfill its function,
        if one is so slippery it willingly sheds its load.

The stepladder empowers a journey to the heights,
     has its feet spread with care,
       with attention to the foundation,
         for strength of posture for its bearing of the load,
         for cross-bracing of the skeleton to prevent a fall,
         for servicing by design the height prescribed.

The staircase serves the will of man,
     is sturdy to withstand two-way traffic,
     has supports of comfort for the hands,
     is well lit at night for safety on the tread,
     is confined in placement for access to the floors,
     is possessed of landings for changes in direction,
         for where the foot is re-aligned,
         for where there is assessment of the pace,
         for where the step is gauged for the foot to fall.

So man can cross and climb with each at variance of purpose
              through selection of the means.

Widespread are the means of man.
Widespread are the selections seen on offer.
Widespread are the solutions devised by man.
Widespread are the ways of man.

Widespread are the offerings of man.

Widespread are the hemlines of his curtaining—
        the hemlines of his garments—
        the hemlines of his leaves.

The means of man measure the widespread abilities of man,
        in order to achieve his objectives of the day,
            his objectives of the night,
            his objectives fulfilled within a life.

The means of man do not enable access to eternal life,
        hold no promise for the future,
        build no portals to the heavens,
        do not have escape pods buried in the pyramids of grandeur.

The means of man have long sought the gods of man,
        have long sought sacrifices for attention,
        have long sought access to a God who answers,
        have long sought extensions to mortality,
        have long sought the means of man for the equipping of a journey
                      into an after-life.

The means of man cannot match the means of God.
The means of man cannot give access to the means of God.
The means of man cannot bear man into the means of God.
The means of man cannot crash-land the means of God.

The means of man tinker with the keys,
        drop them as if a child,
        playing with them yet without understanding:
            the potential within his grasp.

The means of man eventually succumb to chaos,
        disintegrate into the weathered artefacts,
        become as dust upon The Earth which no longer speaks of
            greatness of achievement,
            intimidation of the people,
            misuse of power employed,
            assigning of authority without due care for
                the consequences.

The means of man added the gold of God into their stockpiles,
        the jewels of God into their reservoirs of wealth.

The means of man quickly discovered those which withstood the generations of man,
        seeking to acquire them for his gain—
            yet could not move them past the grave.

The means of man with enlightenment can access the pathway to the stars—
                the pathway for the stars—

cross the river on the stepping stones to the promised land;
climb the staircase with its levels of attainment,
pause on the landings to admire the vistas,
reach the mountaintop with access to the companionship of God.

Beware the many stepladders laid in wait for man,
placed for his temptation to start a climb which can never lead him home,
which end at the doors of cults,
at the doors of idolatry,
at the doors of pyramids,
at the doors which speak of the fallacies of man and of their gods aplenty.

Many are the unique gifts of God:
unique is the offering of God to man;
unique is The God of Love;
unique is The Living God of The Patriarchs;
unique is God's offering of Grace to man in his mortality—
which uplifts him from the grave.

Man,
with his many means,
should embrace within his repertoire his commitment to a new found covenant:
A New Covenant with Grace freely accepted by freewill—
so offered by The God of Love,
as built upon the mainstay of His Cross,
for the family of man."

My Content Study Aid

The Lumps of Clay

"The lumps of clay within the hands of idols could be the lumps of clay within the hands of God.

The lumps of clay upon The Earth can be in the forms of man within The Edifice of God.

The lump of clay which is kicked aside can be the valued child of God lifted high.

The lumps of clay where nothing grows can become the planting of The Lord fruiting in abundance.

The lumps of clay moulded by man according to his will can be the lumps of clay
    destined for the furnace of God—
        to emerge purified and refined—
            creations of great beauty moulded within His will:
                for the assembling of His family.

The lumps of clay do not incur a second glance from man;
    the lumps of clay refined tell of a history of idol worship;
        tell of grace and restoration;
        tell of a new beginning;
        tell of an assured destiny of choice;
        tell of companionship with God.

The lumps of clay need to be reformed;
        need to be transformed;
        need to be the recipients of the washing of the soul;
        need to gush the living water so the thirsty can thereby slake their thirst;
        need to shed their blasphemies with the fitting of new tongues.

The lumps of clay can be embedded with impurities,
        can carry lumps within the lumps,
        can be cracked and dry,
        can be hard and unyielding,
        can be sealed and impervious,
        can be striated and rejected.

The lumps of clay can be treated for imperfections;
        can be suited to reclamation;
        can be recovered;
        can be restored,
        can be saved as worthy;
        can be fitted:
            for the day of salutation,
            for the day of graduation,
            for the day of presentation,
            for the day of registration,

> for the day of embarkation,
> for the day of repatriation,
> for the day of elevation.

The lumps of clay no longer resemble rejected lumps of clay.

The lumps of clay now sparkle as the diamonds,
> are as golden lampstands filled with the anointed oil:
> > flaring with the holy flame of incense in a cascading golden shower.

So the lumps of clay can remain embedded and unmoving,
> or be lifted up to Glow in Glory with The Lighting of The Temples."

My Content Study Aid

The Location of Man

"The location of man is not a happy chance,
        is not the turmoil of creation varying from the laws of agglomeration,
        is not an unselected opportunity awaiting the first signing of life
                complete with instant reproduction.

The location of man removes collisions from within the time frame of man;
        is settled with little variance of heating from the centre of the circling;
        is blessed by a nearby land mass favourable to targeting for exploration:
            as a stepping stone within his own location.

The location of man is blessed with the keeper of the tides and the tilter of the seasons;
        is blessed with the currents of the seas circulating:
                for the benefit of those within the seas,
                      upon the seas,
                      by the seas;
        is blessed by those dependent on the skies who meet the needs of man;
        is blessed by the wholesome lack of predators,
            long since absented from Earth,
                yet fulfilling of their purpose;
        is blessed by the storehouse of The Earth with all which has been laid
                up in preparation:
            for man's time upon The Earth,
        is blessed by the timing for activity and rest as decided by design—
            for an orb to be spun into creation to become The Earth.

The location of man is fitted to his needs,
        not vice versa for contrariness as the fool would postulate.

The location of man is fitted to his size so he can move at ease,
        so he is not stuck upon the ground from which he cannot jump,
        so he is not imprisoned where freewill is not honoured.

The location of man is populated with a great surplus of the chains of life—
        so his dominion may be practised at length:
        letting wisdom eventually surface upon the scenes—
            bearing witness of his imprint.

The location of man is built to witness of His God who waited in the wings;
        who selected His people with great care,
            with great love;
        who gave them edicts by which to live
            so His people would survive:
        while others came and went only to disappear after a short time at the
            forefront of a recorded history.

The location of man is a shining jewel of beauty strung upon the net of gravity:
> in order to display within a void of darkness as a witness of intent.

The location of man has a perspective of grandeur when looked upon from on high,
> has a perspective unimaginable for those who cannot travel,
> has a perspective from the record of those who went before.

The location of man is a home among the stars,
> is a home among the heavens,
> is a home in a place of safety,
> is a home within The Edifice of God.

The location of man does not succumb to interference,
> does not succumb to ageing,
> does not succumb to shortages which cannot be replaced.

The location of man is securely held in the arms of God,
> is part of a larger complex;
> is viewable in all of its intricacy by the eyes of man.

The home of the location of man is available to man,
>> in its fullness of complexity,
>> when in The Eternal Companionship of God.

The home of the location of man views the location of man—
>> as revolving around a distant star in The Firmament of God,
>> as The Showcase of Creation,
>> as The Jewel Box of the Galaxies,
>> as The Epitome of Love Displayed;
>>> where angels long to visit,
>>>> always feel at home,
>>>> always are made welcome."

My Content Study Aid

_____
_____
_____
_____
_____
_____
_____
_____

The Incubators of Man

"The incubation of man is designed to be upon The Earth,
>> is designed to be within the womb,
>> is designed to be within mortality:
>>> exits from the grave as a fledgling of the universe for maturity with God.

The incubation of man imparts wisdom,
>> imparts knowledge of his being,
>> imparts freewill choice,
>> establishes a character,
>> shepherds within a family,
>> disciples within a kingdom,
>> matures for eternity.

The incubation of man,
> the preparation of man,
>> is but a flicker of an eyelid,
>> is but the passing of a gnat,
>> is but a flash of lightning—
as a duration of the time of man when viewed from the prospect of eternity.

The incubators of man are posts of learning with the transmission of understanding,
>> are there to testify in truth,
>> are there not to corrupt the servicing of the growth of man.

The incubators of man should not divert the eyes of man:
>>> from addressing the heavens to a duckpond filled with algae,
>>> from The Morality of God to The Ethics of man,
>>> from the edifice of God to the constructions of man,
>>> from The Truth of God to the lies of man.

The incubators of man should not promote the lie inherent in evolution as if the truth
>>> of man—
>> until each promoter can reproduce the trial,
>> with nothing but the chemicals of Earth before the dawn of life,
>> thereby bringing to pass the creation of life itself:
>>> within the reproductive species which need to grow and feed.

Beware the incubators of random theories based on the evolution of man.

Beware of those forsaking,
> when it suits them,
>> the relationship of cause and effect within the time lines established by man:
>>> for his attempting understanding of The Mysteries of God.

Beware the charlatans who start with life established,
>   who dissect it for a splice,
>   who would seek to cheat their ways into the halls of fame.

Beware the risks to the disruption of the stability of life as man meddles for his season—
>   in things beyond his measure of control or comprehension.

Beware the ore within The Earth with its potential to become a bicycle,
>   without a designer and constructor so the ore remains as ore,
>   where cause and effect are no longer treated as a wedded pair.

Beware the bicycle when left alone decays back to its ore to lie again amongst the dust.

Beware of the facets of creation which pre-empt the whole of man's reality based
>   as arising—
>   within unaided time alone—
>   from the soup,
>   within a kitchen without guidance,
>   and to thereby attain the magnificence:
>   of being self-aware.

For such as this defies the logic of simplicity,
>   as man,
>   forsaking common sense,
>   promotes his theorem of evolution as a fact of life:
>   his theorem of the species which cannot self-start;
>   his theorem which fails to create the hinge of life on which
>   the theorem swings;
>   his theorem with no flashpoint of ignition,
>   no fuel on which to feed;
>   his theorem without a basal cause:
>   recording via observation a preferential part of the assumed effect,
>   and interpolates the rest."

My Content Study Aid

The Embarking on A Journey

"Embarking on a journey is sometimes not easy to achieve,
               is sometimes fraught with perils,
               is sometimes needing of resources,
               is sometimes out of time,
               is sometimes not worth the effort,
               is sometimes retracing footsteps,
               is sometimes very rewarding to the spirit and the soul:
                             with a sojourn in a land of wonders.

Embarking on a journey requires foresight for the laws of man,
               requires insight for the counselling of God.

Embarking on a journey speaks of the distant lands of man,
               speaks of the promised land of God.

Embarking on a journey bespeaks a destination where the soul desires to wander,
               where the spirit has a preference.

Embarking on a journey may preclude return,
               may lead forever onwards,
               may continue past the gates of praise,
                         past the courts of praise.

Embarking on a journey can satisfy a longing,
               can satisfy a quest for sourcing distant images,
               can satisfy the search for living water from the oases fed by God.

Embarking on a journey testifies of a commitment,
               verifies an intent,
               so defies the gainsayers and the soothsayers who would inhibit.

Embarking on a journey should excite both the soul and the spirit—
                             in the absence of trepidation.

Embarking on a journey can bring into achievement the desires of the heart,
                       the inspections of the soul,
                       the victory of the spirit—
                       with the close companionship of God.

Embarking on a journey may see a grave approaching,
               may see a grave receding,
               may see the mournful drying eyes,
               may see the once mournful laughing in The Son-light.

Embarking on a journey is best put into the hands of God,
               is best left for the vistas known to God,

is best walked by A Temple infused with The Spirit of
The Living God.

Embarking on a journey should be prepared to note the way stations of The Lord—
the turning points of life;
the divine appointments;
the testimonies and solace;
the sighting of the signs and wonders;
the participation in the miracles of God—
those which may not have been presented in the absence of the body soul and spirit:
prevented from embarking.

Embarkation is the tipping point of God;
is when His Spirit goes before—
is kept busy with the doors;
is when grace flows in abundance and the sufferers know rest;
is when the healing balm of Gilead pervades—
and pain is vanquished with its signing of intent.

Behold:
when God smiles upon His people and meets them in their tents;
when God blesses His people and shows them through His Temples;
when God promises His people of a destiny and accompanies them on their way."

My Content Study Aid

_____
_____
_____
_____
_____
_____
_____
_____
_____
_____
_____
_____
_____
_____
_____

The Seeping of The Blood

"The seeping of the blood goes from red to black,
        goes from sticky to a solid,
        goes from the landscapes of man to The Temples of The Lord.

The seeping of the blood is inexorable once started,
        is from an unimpeded flow,
        is a testimony to the folly unleashed by man.

The seeping of the blood speaks of life extinguishing,
        speaks of lack of movement of the source,
        speaks of the absence of The Living offering help.

The seeping of the blood tells of a story filled with carnage,
        a story filled with blood-letting,
        a story with no mercy granted as a last resort.

The seeping of the blood is everywhere encountered,
        is on the evening news of man,
        is on the lips of those who revel in the gore.

The seeping of the blood is shed without an end in sight,
        is shed upon the whim of man,
        is shed upon the shielded plans of man.

The seeping of the blood creeps up to the shoes which move away,
        creeps up to the crevices which fill,
        creeps up to a barrier in place.

The seeping of the blood creeps until the source no longer pumps,
        until the flow has levelled out,
        until the tide no longer ebbs.

The seeping of the blood is not intended so to be,
        is not intended to be viewed,
        is not intended to sign the end of life.

The seeping of the blood signs of the breaking of the moral laws of God,
        signs of violence rendered to the creation of God,
        signs of accountability required from each holder of the cause.

The seeping of the blood is seen in the receptacles of disposal,
        is seen upon the floor set for invasion,
        is seen upon a bed where embryos have life,
                where foetuses are fused to be exploded,
                where birthing still would wait in preparation.

The seeping of the blood halts with the stopping of the heartbeat—

upon consent of the entrusted mother
yet not to be as such;
with the stopping of the heartbeat—
despite the viewed struggle for survival;
with the stopping of the heartbeat—
in defiance of The God of Love.

The seeping of the blood is to the shame of man,
is to the currency of the blood oaths issued,
is to join the blood tide generated by those who honour not—
a sacred trust.

The seeping of the blood marks each sacrifice in vain,
each forced sacrifice without consent,
each ending sacrifice which brings no honour to the dead.

The seeping of the blood is recorded by the angels,
when an instance,
within the record of each man;
is recorded for use within the coming presence of man;
is recorded so accountability can be summoned to the halls of justice;
is recorded with allocation to the wisdom of God."

My Content Study Aid

_____
_____
_____
_____
_____
_____
_____
_____
_____
_____
_____
_____
_____
_____
_____

My Children of The World

"My children of the world can set The World on Fire:
>>can speak the golden tongues,
>>can bear the golden testimonies,
>>can win the golden souls.

My children of the world are My ambassadors at large:
>>My ambassadors with messages,
>>My ambassadors with conviction,
>>My ambassadors with answers.

My children of the world are My ambassadors with the golden touch,
>>>with the golden gifts,
>>>with The Golden Spirit to make known.

My children of the world pray the golden prayers for others,
>>seek the golden counselling,
>>know the golden presence of The Lord.

My children of the world hearken to the golden moment,
>>call upon the golden hosts,
>>receive the golden visions,
>>drink of the golden cup filled with water from the golden river:
>>>>which always flows to life.

My children of the world have the golden manners,
>>have the golden tasks,
>>have the golden blessings from The Lord.

My children of the world prepare to be The Golden Bride,
>>wait for the golden dawn—
>>>to receive a golden welcome to the golden shores.

My children of the world are the golden archetypes of willing golden servants,
>>are the golden forerunners of a golden kingdom,
>>are the golden torch bearers of a golden flame.

  For such as these will never tarnish,
>>are repositories of great value,
>>are magnificent to see in action,
>>are a wonder to behold.

  For such as these will never fade away,
>>never rot away,
>>never be hidden out of sight.

  For such as these are nurtured and tended by the hosts of Heaven:

as their colours change from black through all the greys unto the white:
and then begin to sparkle—
as the golden jewels of each passage through mortality—
are fitted to each golden gown of life."

My Content Study Aid

The Storm of The Wealth of Man

"Behold,
       the storm of the wealth of man gathers as the dust clouds in the desert,
              gathers the pressure cells in combination,
              gathers the despair of man for circulation on The Earth.

The storm of the wealth of man awaits the pressure build-up,
            awaits the festering and the spreading of concern,
            awaits the wind change from within the deserts bringing
                      dust unto all the seas.

The storm of the wealth of man is building on the debt of man perceived as due
                                      to be dishonoured,
          on the indebted paper of a nation accumulated in the east,
          on the debt of a nation where no-one wants its paper,
          on the debt of a nation whose collateral is out of reach
                              of creditors,
          on the debt of a nation who uses its printing press—
                to paper over the cracks growing by the day.

The storm of the wealth of man is a storm of self-destruction,
        is a storm with repeated echoes,
            is a storm which blows the paper of man before it in the dust:
                        where no-one picks it up.

The storm of the wealth of man is the outpouring of a loss of faith,
              the final surfacing of what has become the time
                              of unbelief,
            the opening of the barn doors as the hoarding,
                      infested with the nests,
                      is expelled together with the rats and mice.

The storm of the wealth of man reaches the final tipping point as the storm demolishes
      the houses built with cards,
      the paper trails which move in circles,
      the signatures not called to account for the end result,
      the artful use of paper whose value no longer is able to be established,
                whose value only makes it fit for origami.

The storm of the wealth of man ends with dreams in tatters,
              ends with retirement plans destroyed,
              ends with false wisdom after the event.

The storm of the wealth of man envelops all within the dustball out in front,
            catches the herd completely unaware still enmeshed in promises,
            catches the bulls upon the cattle stops of driveways to the mansions,

    catches cows upon the cowcatchers at the forefront of the freight trains,
    catches the slickest and the slowest before they have the time to move,
    catches the greedy and the foolish with their stockpiles unprotected:
        their stockpiles which wither as they watch.

The storm of the wealth of man breaks upon the moving of a second hand
        upon a timepiece held by man,
  is in full flood well before the closing bell of desperation,
  resurges at the day break of new venues frozen in the fright,
  overcomes the barriers intended for protection of the bank roll of a nation,
  surges round The Earth gathering momentum—
      as the shops put up their shutters,
      as the shops call out to the landlords,
      as the shops go up for sale,
      as the shops are seen to have no back-stops:
      for when the emperor is seen to have no clothes.

The storm of the wealth of man brings the castles tumbling to The Earth;
    lets the moats be forded when the water is seen to be but ankle deep;
    lets the gates be opened as the inhabitants surrender before the folly
        evident as undressed—
      with the discovering of the myth propounded;
    lets the ransacking of the castles continue unabated—
      as the lemmings of the world of finance rush unto the cliffs
        knowing there are no ladders down.

The storm of the wealth of man has the speed of conquest,
    defies the speed of man,
  is tied to the tail-end of the shadow as it is seen to cross The Earth.

The storm of the wealth of man has horrific consequences on the seats of commerce:
    in the thorough loss of trust;
    in the widespread suspicion of the folding coinage of the
        sovereign realms;
    in the demanding of repayment of all the forms of debt;
    in the loss of value bound to all collateral within the
        instruments of exchange.

The storm of the wealth of man is held in check as it bypasses—
    looks on from a distance without touching or infringing—
    the golden sheen in safe keeping;
    the golden metal with a history of success in trade;
    the golden target which paces the spiking of inflation,
      which defies the cutting edge of deflation;
    the storm-proof golden holder of the value of the day:
    the safe and golden harbour holding the gold of God.

  Wise is man,

    wise are the saints:
        who know the gold of God is held safely un-pledged within each storehouse—
            able to withstand the firestorms affecting the wealth of man:
                when the paper inscribed by man is not worth the chasing,
                      is not worth the catching,
                          as it blows away.

The storm of the wealth of man teeters within its own gestation;
        as the machines of man spit out the ink-demanding balances of numbers;
        as qualified by the trailing zeros which man can no longer count unaided,
                can no longer redeem,
                can no longer swap,
                can no longer sell,
        can no longer either value or access the collateral of the day—
            as it changes by the night.

Foolish indeed are they who sleep without concern for what the day will bring.
Foolish are they who procrastinate their way to ruin.
Foolish are those driven by the quest for wealth without the knowledge of the market:
        in which they choose to play.

Wise are those who pursue their visions in linkage with the hand of God,
        in linkage with the counsel of His Spirit,
        in linkage with the destiny of wonder."

My Content Study Aid

_____
_____
_____
_____
_____
_____
_____
_____
_____
_____
_____
_____
_____

The Crossing of The Threshold

"The crossing of the threshold is instantaneous when within mortality,
    is as a night of sleep when within the grave,
    is with assistance from the angels when aborted from
              the womb.

The crossing of the threshold starts as a step of faith,
    ends as a leap of knowledge.

The crossing of the threshold sets aside the cares of man,
    changes the assessment of his wealth,
    rewards the step of faith into the realm of God.

The crossing of the threshold is a one-way trip,
    has no ticket for return unless with a visa as a visitor.

The crossing of the threshold enlivens the fullness of the memory of man in his mortality,
    in his prior dwelling as a spirit in the confines of God.

The crossing of the threshold makes visible each gown of life,
    makes visible all the other beings—
      both of hearsay and of acquaintance—
who step the great divide between the three life experiences of man.

The crossing of the threshold is not a lonely state,
    has no time to register,
    has no time at all.

The crossing of the threshold takes differing paths for My sheep and for his goats.

The crossing of the threshold does not succumb to error in procedure,
    to error in the destiny as dependent on the freewill of man.

The crossing of the threshold is as the crossing of the river into the promised land.

The crossing of the threshold displays the vista of The Tree of Life.

The crossing of the threshold is as the birthing from the grave—
    with the baptism from The Father for the blessing of His Son.

The crossing of the threshold speaks of the abilities of God reserved for His creation,
    not to stand as a lonely functionary with no purpose to evolvement,
    but as a fully fledged progression to attainment of all God would bestow."

My Content Study Aid

The Writings of God

"The writings of God are not submitted to man to give him something with which to
                                            argue back and forth,
            are not for the bringing of divisions,
            are not for the violent defending of The Faith in God.

The writings of God are to impart knowledge of God,
                        of His concern for man,
                        of His belief in man,
                        of His companionship with man,
                        of His sacrifice for man,
                        of His reconciliation of man with God,
        of His being both in the reality of man and in the presence of the sacred.

The writings of God testify of God's interaction with man in his glory in righteousness
                                                        and truth,
                with man in his shame as his head is
                                hung with downcast eyes.

The writings of God record His dealing with those who stand in confrontation against
                                        His people and His being:
        as the ill-treatments are heaped on the mistreatments of His people,
        as blasphemies intermingle in a three-way tie with The Father,
                                                The Son,
                                        and The Holy Spirit—
                where the three are one and the one is three.

The writings of God testify of a history proclaimed in detail:
            a history not purged of the failings of man;
            a history not purged of the wrath of God falling within His vengeance;
            a history not purged of the laws of God with the rebellion of man;
            a history not purged of the sacrifice of God with His gift of grace.

The writings of God give ample guidance to The Truth,
            give ample guidance with due warnings,
            give ample guidance as to the intent of God.

The writings of God are recorded as intended,
            stand as intended,
            declare as intended—
                    in their survival within the mixing of the politics of man.

The writings of God reach above the hatred of man,
            reach above the love of man,
            reach above the godlessness of man,
            reach above the godliness of man,

reach above to shower all with His grace who share a contrite heart.

The writings of God are not silenced by the edicts of man,
    are not transformed by the vilifications of man,
    are not aborted by the blood of martyrs,
    are not dissembled by the raging fires of books,
    are not overcome by the arbitrary laws of man.

The writings of God stand in righteousness and truth,
    are upheld by God,
    distil the truth for perception from the lies,
    have prophecies to the fore for this day and age,
    change lives upon a reading with effect on generations,
    hold the keys to gifts within the reality of man,
    proclaim My Spirit's guidance to the spirit for the soul,
    speak of My Spirit's coming,
    speak of the witnessing of miracles—
            all through the centuries of man,
              within an epoch of His writings,
              for the benefit of man.

The writings of God carry an intense intent:
    carry messages both sublime and flagrant,
    carry messages of both rejection and encouragement,
        of both war and peace,
        of both loyalty and betrayal.

The writings of God are secured under the hand of God,
    are testifying through My Holy Spirit,
    are enfranchised with My Spirit's call,
    are protected by The Father within The Edifice of The Son of God."

My Content Study Aid

_____
_____
_____
_____
_____
_____
_____
_____
_____

The Sky Signs of God

"The rainbow of God is well known by man,
        is well known by God,
            is remindful of a promise to the forbears of the generations
                      presently upon The Earth.

The rainbow of God is not the only repeating sign of God seen within the skies above the
                      heads of man—
            as being ever mindful of His overseeing presence.

The rainbow of God is seen,
        as a multi-coloured bow arched in the sky,
                by man as stationed on The Earth.

The rainbow of God is seen,
        as a perfect circle centred on the eye of man,
                by man as stationed to look down.

The rainbow of God is a marriage of the sun and rain,
        so to lift the spirit of man nearer to His God.

The rainbow of God forswears the company of both the Northern and the Southern lights
                      by night.

The Northern and the Southern Lights are the auroras of The Earth imparted with both
                      grace and beauty.

The auroras of The Earth sign of man's protection on his flight through space,
        guard the welfare of man's being,
        guard the ark of God man uses both for transport through the seasons
                and for the living space on board.

The auroras of The Earth are the curtains of delight with the rhythm of cascading light
            spread before the eyes of man:
      synchronized according to the chorister of the dance;
        according to the baton of the music maker of the heavens;
        according to the composition of God—
            as presented for His children to watch in awe.

The auroras of The Earth come and go according to the heart-beat of the sun,
                  to the pulses of the sun;
      sign all is well for the stars on-board as the ark glides on her course.

The auroras of The Earth are in company with the shooting stars homing on The Earth;
    see the shooting stars trailing their life-force through the heavens but to fall,
      sight the being of the shooting stars for but an instance saying, here am I,
              as they flash into oblivion—

joining with The Earth as she continues on her journey.

The shooting stars are long term travellers meeting with their destiny,
> keeping an appointment known to God,
>> fulfilling a scheduled timetable to enliven the night sky of God—
>>> for His viewers of distinction.

The shooting stars of God are sprinkled from His pepper pot to meet a fiery end.

The comets are the prey of giants:
> drawn in to their predators,
> make an imprint when they strike,
> have no time for dwarfs.

The comets are structured on their journeys:
> return according to their long set paths,
> continue on beyond the scope of watching eyes as their tails
>> commence to shrink.

Beware the giants of God as they scavenge all the offerings to feed a voracious maw.

Beware the giants of God as the sweepers of the skies,
> the sink-holes for collisions,
> the caretakers of the errant screamers—
>> which test the safety nets of God.

Beware the giants of God for they care not for what they eat:
> consume all there is on offer,
> will not release once trapped,
> are happy with a burp.

The flashes and the claps are destined for the eyes and ears of man.

The flashes and the claps warn man from a distance of potential to approach;
> warn man of a change within the cloud base of the skies;
> warn man to seek some shuttered shelter of protection;
> warn man of an approach as frequency increases,
>> as the time of separation decreases with the distance.

The flashes and the claps relate to energy released,
> relate to a short circuit to The Earth,
> relate to the need for wisdom on where to decide to stand.

The flashes and the claps can hold man spell-bound with amazement:
> as the lightning lights the sky,
> as the thunder diminishes in rolling echoes of its birth,
> as man stands frozen to a spot and may forget to run.

The flashes and the claps sign of a storm released,
> of a storm building for a downpour,
> of a storm seething within itself as it readies to freeze or soak.

The coming of the day at sunrise,
  the setting of the sun at end-of-day,
    sign the time frame passing in an instant in which The Master of creation
          applies His grandeur to His Clouds of Glory,
      applies as with a brush stippled from His selections among
      The Colourings of God:
      The Colourings which set the sky aflame;
        The Colourings which have man gaze in awe at the beauty he beholds;
     have man watch intently until the blues and greys again dominate—
          the memory of a majestic spectacle.

  A spectacle of God preceding sunrise in the dawn,
      succeeding sunset in the twilight of the day.

The rising and the setting of the sun witness the masterpiece of decoration created
            for the skies—
      through the skilful touch of the hand of God—
        as He places His brushstrokes on His canvas
           composed from His tableau of the clouds.

The sky signs of God are numerous and specific,
      are widespread and majestic,
      are memorable and marvellous.

The sky signs of God testify of His creation:
      of His thought and planning,
      of His structures and displays,
      of His control and timing.

The sky signs of God await The Blood-red Colouring,
    await The Darkening of The Brightness—
        as to be laid before the eyes of man."

My Content Study Aid

_____
_____
_____
_____
_____
_____
_____

The Boundaries of The Earth

"The boundaries of The Earth were never there for man's containment,
        were never known until he reached out to the stars,
        were never within his span of knowledge until his libraries
                were filled.

The boundaries of The Earth bring disquiet to some.

The boundaries of The Earth are the seas between the lands,
        are the mountains to be passed,
        are the winds to be conquered,
        are the safe harbours to be found,
        are the steep climbs to space where freedom also waits,
        are the engines needing fuelling.

The boundaries of The Earth are the rivers without crossings,
        are the chasms to be bridged,
        are the roads yet to be built,
        are the search for food,
        are the warring of the nations,
        are the solitudes of environments not conducive to man.

The boundaries of The Earth are not fenced by God,
        are sometimes fenced by man,
        are not set with alarms by God,
        are sometimes alarmed by man.

The boundaries of The Earth reach out into space,
        reach into the depths,
        reach where the sunlight does not go,
                does not carry heat,
                does not warm the darkness.

The boundaries of The Earth reach out to where the intersects meet with the death zones
                              of man—
    whether designed and laid by God or designed and laid by man.

The boundaries of The Earth are subject to the strivings of man,
        to the intent of man,
        to the freewill of man.

The boundaries of The Earth are not for the sequestering of man.

The boundaries of The Earth are as challenges to man:
                for him to overcome,
                for him to put a ribbon on a chest,
                for him to put a trophy on a wall,

>   for him to put an image in a book,
>   for him to gather treasure for his vault.

The boundaries of The Earth are shared by God with man."

My Content Study Aid

The Capacity of Man

"The capacity of man is not a measure of his size,
        is not a gauging of his limits,
            is not an absorption of his details.

The capacity of man speaks of his prospects for development,
                his grappling with success,
                his handling of the worldly pride.

The capacity of man is known to God,
        is understood by God,
        is installed through God.

The capacity of man has a brain sized for great things,
                for the achieving of his dreams,
                for the reaching out beyond his body,
                for the grasping of his goals,
                for the understanding of eternity,
                for his passage through the portals,
                for the presence of transforming grace.

The capacity of man does not progress to wonders when rejecting of Grace, does
        not use the stepping stones when a stone is missing, does
        not complete the journey when the goal is ill-defined,
                when the goal is un-defined,
                when the goal is non-defined,
                when the goal is stuck still on the default.

The capacity of man can enhance his objectives,
        can enhance his vision for his life,
        can enhance the options from the bronze through silver to the gold of man;
from the clay through lead unto the bronze past iron to silver then the gold of God.

The capacity of man is not attained in fullness when failure is expected,
                when churlishness sustains,
                when the spirit hears the whimpers of the soul.

The capacity of man is sealed with the promises of God behind a golden door;
        needs The Golden Latchkey of Faith to open wide the access:
                through into the mansion of the promises.

The capacity of man knows no bounds when liberated from enslavement,
        when set free on the pathway to discovery,
        when walking in discipleship with
                The Spirit's leading.

The capacity of man is open-ended,

is unlimited,
is from tlie foresight of Tlie Loving God."

My Content Study Aid

A Love Note to My Children

"A love note to My children is as a song birthed and freed within The Stars of God,
        is a song committed between hearts,
        is a song which only those with love can sing,
        is a song of goodness sent to smiling hearts in tune.

A love note to My children is a song within a song:
        is the song which never ends within the song of action,
        is the song of inspiration within the song of tenderness,
        is the song of love within the song of sacrifice,
        is The Bridal Song within the song of Vows,
        is the song of laughter within the song of joy,
        is the song of man within the song of God.

A love note to My children is written on each heart,
        is spoken by My Spirit to each spirit awake and well,
        is heard by each soul attuned to The Will of God.

A love note to My children carries a reminder of an appointment:
            the promise of return;
            the proximity of the wedding;
            the presence at the wedding feast;
            the departure of the earthbound;
    the arrival of the earthbound unto the presence of the being of man;
    the arrival of the earthbound unto the presence of their God.

A love note to My children carries a reminder to be ready,
        to be prepared,
        to be certain of the gown selected—
      clean and pressed and ready—
            for the soul already washed and bathed,
            for the spirit filled to overflowing.

A love note to My children warns of no disruptions,
        warns of no going back for that which is not brought,
      warns of the need to dress correctly for entrance to The Bridegroom,
            for access to The Altar of The Lamb,
            for progression unto The Enthroned of God.

A love note to My children is signed and sealed by God,
        confirms an invitation extended long ago,
        is valued for uplifting from His table whereon His body and
                            His blood do rest."

Faith Filled Faithful Servants

"Faith filled faithful servants are hard to enlist,
                are scarce upon the ground,
                are worthy to be praised.

Faith filled faithful servants seek and find that which is difficult to possess—
                                            The Trust of God.

Faith filled faithful servants attend to the finest detail,
                      with alacrity and purpose,
                      with the goal for achievement set on as
                            near a perfect outcome as abilities permit.

Faith filled faithful servants are as the sentinels of God,
                are as reliable as the sun rise,
                are as plentiful as rubies,
                are the stokers of the fires of God.

Faith filled faithful servants are the tall poppies of God,
                      who can see distant horizons,
                      who can envisage the need before requested,
                      who are never placed in vases,
                      who are encouraged to grow taller,
                      who are in company with God,
                      who are in the most rewarding of relationships.

Faith filled faithful servants are the firewalls of protection,
                are the emitters of encouragement,
                are the transferors of the gifts.

Faith filled faithful servants come and go within The Will of God,
                come and go with The Tongues of Heaven,
                come and go in the experience of miracles,
                      in the sighting of the wonders,
                      in the knowledge of the signs,
                      in the carrying of the keys.

Faith filled faithful servants never whisper secrets,
                never speak behind another's back,
                never utter lies,
                never are harnessed under pride.

Faith filled faithful servants have souls accustomed to honouring the spirit,
                      to listening intently to The Holy Spirit,
                      to marking each day with prayer in a conversation
                                      with their living God.

Anthony A Eddy (Scribe)

Faith filled faithful servants have little need to query,
                          have little need to ascertain,
                          have little need to verify,
                          have little need to mount a session filled with questions,
                          have little need for adulation,
                          have little need for congratulation.

Faith filled faithful servants are knowledgeable of The Ways of God,
                          know well The Fear of God,
                          always bring Honour to The Table.

Faith filled faithful servants refuse to discuss the trivial,
                          refuse to recount a downfall,
                          refuse to throw accelerants onto a smoking pile.

Faith filled faithful servants refuse to participate in the confusions of man,
                          refuse to stir a muddied pool,
                          refuse to listen to a babel,
                          refuse to speculate at random,
                          refuse to retreat from light,
                          refuse to be unequally yoked.

Faith filled faithful servants can be trusted with their promises,
                          can be trusted for completion,
                          can be trusted with the sacred,
                          can be trusted within The Edifice of God,
                          can be trusted with The Gold of God,
                          can be trusted to manage and achieve each heart's intent.

Faith filled faithful servants know the value of appointments,
                          the time within the day of man,
                          the time required to travel,
                          the time set for arrival,
                          the time due for departure that does not outstay
                                                      a welcome.

Faith filled faithful servants do not grimace in a silence,
                          do not infringe on social boundaries,
                          do not heap food upon a plate,
                          do not revisit until all are seen to have a plate in hand.

Faith filled faithful servants do not lag behind,
                          accomplish the content of their taskings,
                          do not deal in trite excuses without the weight of truth,
                          do not bring a null report when it is out of time.

Faith filled faithful servants listen and confirm,
                          action and achieve,
                          finish and await.

Faith filled faithful servants are The Ambassadors of God,
> The Envoys of The Lord,
> The Close Friends of The Spirit,
> The Saints seen with their missions—
>> whether close by or far afield—
>> which contribute to The Edifice of God."

My Content Study Aid

The God of Man

"The vitality of man has seen man birthed and multiplied,
            has seen him established with dominion,
            has seen him king of his technology,
            has seen him reaching for the stars,
            has seen him attempting to farewell his God.

The God of man is his originator,
            is his sequencer,
            is his reconciler,
            is his redeemer,
            is his saviour,
            is his provider,
            is his source of grace.

The God of man is unique within eternity,
            is jealous and formidable,
            is the maker of man in His own image,
            is loving and uplifting,
            is the only God of man alive and caring for His people,
            is the God who answers prayers,
            is the God with supremacy over all and every thing.

The God of man encircles the world of man,
            leaves no bolt hole in which to hide,
            leaves no path open for escape.

The God of man encompasses the being of man,
            knows the stone to turn when searching,
            knows the tempter's power defeated,
            knows The Pathway to The Cross,
            knows The Pathway to The Father,
            knows The Building Block of Faith,
            knows The Pathway to The Son.

The God of man counsels and determines,
            chastens and curtails,
            enlightens and envelops.

The God of man is the surrogate of parenthood,
            is the harbinger of Grace,
            is the worker of The Miracles.

The God of man opens up the wonders,
            declares what is to be,
            wills the sharing of inheritance.

The God of man festoons the heavens with the signs,
        highlights the beauties of renown,
        shares His space with man.

The God of man dispatches evil to be sequestered,
        discharges those infected from his presence,
        denies those who insist on clinging to what should be foregone.

The God of man does not insinuate Himself,
        does not impose Himself,
        does not thunder in coercion,
        does not infringe the freewill of man.

The God of man is the seeker of relationships,
        is for the living and the loving,
        is the source of all His gifts.

The God of man is the secretor of His tears for the waywardness of man;
        is the sender of His Spirit to comfort and relate;
        is the descriptor of the universe unto the senses of man;
        is the installer of The Cross as impressed on the memory of man;
        is The Bridegroom-in-waiting for His Bride;
        is The Be-all of Fear and Worship within the existence of man;
        is The God of Ages made known upon The Earth."

My Content Study Aid

The Scenery of God Abroad

"The scenery of man prepares for expansion as man
                         takes in the scenery of God and man at home,
                         takes in the scenery of God abroad.

The scenery of God abroad requires more senses of man,
                his ability to handle what presently lies beyond his reach:
    more deftness in perception so he can gauge and judge correctly;
    more resolution for the new scoping of his eyes;
    more frequencies for the new scoping of his ears;
    more keys to unlock the new senses for the evaluating of new dimensions;
    more techniques of exploration for the coping with new dimensions—
                      both for the very small and for the very large;
    more enhancing of the senses with which he is familiar;
    more practicality in travelling the outer islands which man has never seen
                              before close up and unafraid,
        in travelling the white holes of God—
            where mass no longer interferes,
            where short cuts are employed,
            where light has no need to sign to its companions.

The scenery of God abroad has the angels gasping,
        has the angels silenced,
        has the angels moving slowly and in awe.

The scenery of God abroad implies visits to the lands of wonder,
                to the lands of monuments,
                to the lands of spectacles,
                to the lands of giants,
                to the lands of microcosms,
                to the lands of joy,
                to the lands of progress.

The scenery of God abroad is vested within the deeds of God,
            is vested within the grandest of designs,
            is vested within The Blessings and The Power of God.

The scenery of God abroad is beautiful,
            is delightful,
            is seasonal,
            is conceptual,
            is majestic,
            is grandeur on a scale unknown to man:
            is being shared within The Family of God.

The scenery of God abroad does not lend itself to disappointment,
>> is assessed as being well worth the waiting,
>> holds sights forever on the curricula of man,
>> is sighted as assignments worth repeat appraisals,
>> is honoured as the outpourings from The God of Love,
>> is preserved within the scenes where time is known to visit
>>>> and then to leave.

The scenery of God abroad is accepted as The Works of God,
>> as the working of His Spirit in foreign jurisdictions—
>>>> where man has never gone,
>> as The Manifested Will of God in being—
>>>> and disclosed.

The scenery of God abroad speaks of distant lands and venues in other realms of God,
>> speaks of the imprints of God which cannot be eclipsed,
>> speaks of The Preparations of God—
>>>> those which He made for His Family at Home to visit."

My Content Study Aid

The Awakening of My People

"The awakening of My people unfolds with The Approaching of The Day.

The Glory of My people falls as they arise.
The blessing of My people is from The Father's Hand.
The raising of My people is by instructions from The Throne.
The dressing of My people is guided by My angels.
The purity of My people is essential for My Bride.
The sanctity of My people stands in righteousness.

The day of the awakening is sure and bespoke,
                is hallowed and honoured,
                is checked and not found wanting.

The day of the awakening is prepared for and determined,
                is vibrant and appealing,
                is glorious and grateful.

The day of the awakening is active and ascending,
                is beautiful and bountiful,
                is conscious and consuming.

The day of the awakening is justified and sacred,
                is profound and prolific,
                is personal and presenting.

The day of the awakening supervises and selects,
                endears and endeavours,
                achieves and reflects.

The arising in glory completes and fulfils,
                is called and foreseen,
                applies destinies and confirms,
                initiates and transfers,
                activates and uplifts,
                is seen and envied.

The Father's Hand of blessing is extended and hovers,
                      validates and welcomes,
                      secures and adopts,
                      touches and imparts,
                      seeks and includes,
                      progresses and shares,
                      speaks and endows.

Instructions from The Throne are directed and directive,

                      are simple and constrained,
                      are loving and gentle,
                      are precise and understood,
                      are timely and consistent,
                      are sacred and solicitous,
                      are obeyed and completed.

My angels' guidance in dressing is inspection and approval,
                      is fitting and flowing,
                      is touching and appreciating.

My angels' guidance in dressing supervises and corrects,
                      embellishes and decorates,
                      enhances and scintillates.

My angels' guidance in dressing is scoping and surveying,
                      is turning and checking,
                      is fastidious and particular.

My angels' guidance in dressing is memorable and long-lasting,
                      is unhurried and thorough,
                      is comfortable and acceptable.

My angels' guidance in dressing is sequenced and in-tune,
                      is thoughtful and experienced,
                      is masterful and discerning.

My angels' guidance in dressing is permanent and tasteful,
                      is magnificent and joyful,
                      is majestic and triumphant.

My angels' guidance in dressing is forthcoming and mature,
                      is rewarding and appraising,
                      is glorious and final.

The bridal fitting of My people knows the reflections and the lighting,
                      the offerings and the gowns,
                      the garlands and the crowns.

The bridal fitting of My people knows the quest for purity and the walk of righteousness,
                      sounds the bells of jubilation and hears the call of distant trumpets,
                      visits the hall of mirrors and commits all to the memory.

The bridal fitting of My people chooses from the bouquets of grandeur and the music to
                                              the altar,
                      chooses the backdrop to the scene and the betrothal ring,
                      chooses the guard of honour and the attendants for the day.

The bridal fitting of My people chooses the headdress for the star and the train of plenty,
                      chooses the arm of reassurance and the arms of guidance,

    chooses from a treasure chest and from the shoes of completion.

The bridal fitting of My people is an affair of grandeur and an affair of function,
    is the terminal of preparation and the interval—
        before the venue is fully filled,
    is the star time for the music maker
        and for the songsters of eternity.

The bridal fitting of My people is readied for assembly and for the orchestration,
    is prepared to mount a dais and to stand before the altar,
    is awaiting and ready for the cueing.

My people know redemption and salvation,
  know the sacred and the sanctified,
  know faith and righteousness.

My people live by the word and the promises,
    by the testimonies and the blood as shed,
    by the visions and the prophets.

My people serve and go,
  live and do,
  hear and minister.

My people respond and seek,
  uplift and encourage,
  share and invite.

My people spread and proclaim,
  carry and dispense,
  master and transmit.

My people usher and teach,
  care for and protect,
  graduate and prosper.

My people of the covenant,
    whether new or old,
      are all welcome to approach their loving God,
      are all welcome to seek the making of amends,
      are all welcome to be washed for a new beginning.

My people are known and qualified for receiving The Grace within My favour,
        The Grace within My presence,
        The Grace within the age of pentecost revealed."

The Way Stations of The Lord

"The stations of the cross result from the honouring by My people—
$$\text{in their times of mourning.}$$

The stations of the cross are not intended to be so.

The stations of the cross mark the road to victory,
        mark the road to Calvary,
        mark the road to reconciliation of man and God.

The stations of the cross are misplaced when on a street map,
        should be placed within The Temple of My Spirit,
        should be welcomed and attended.

The stations of the cross are the way stations of The Lord when within mortality.

The Lamb's Book of Life welcomes the entries of the way stations of The Lord on the
        street map of the soul.

The way stations of the Lord may not be present on the street map of a soul,
        may not be present on the indexing of a spirit,
        may not be present with an impact on the body.

The way stations of The Lord are numerous and consensual:
        as entered on the street map of the soul,
        as entered in the indexing of the spirit,
        as entered for renewal of the body.

The way stations of The Lord complete within the temple,
        are partial while the sun keeps rising on the temple,
        are completed upon the final sunset on an entered grave.

The way stations of The Lord comprise:
    the birth from within the womb of celebration;
    the sprouting of the seed of faith;
    the committing of the body soul and spirit as the house becomes transformed —
        into a temple;
    the immersion of obedience with the new birth of the body soul and spirit;
    the blessing of the gifts as they are discovered;
    the freeing of the tongue from blasphemy—
        so the tongues of Heaven may come forth;
    the service inherent in each tasking and the pause between;
    the frequent participation before the table of The Lord:
        where the bread and wine,
        as ascribed to time,
        are shared at each remembrance—
        where prior repentance is the highlight as added sin is so forsworn,

where the slate of life obtains erasure under My mantling of grace;
the entry and the passing to and through the grave.

The way stations of The Lord are each a place of rest,
        are each a place of prayer,
        are each a place of victory:
    for the confirmation of the progress of the soul.

The way stations of The Lord are the stepping stones encountered on the way to
                                            eternal life,
        are the turning points at life events,
        are the road signs offered at the cross roads,
                offered at the intersections,
                offered at the junctions of decision."

My Content Study Aid

The Twisting of The Tongue of Man

"The twisting of the tongue of man is a serious condition,
                         needs immediate attention,
                         requires an urgent fix.

The twisting of the tongue of man originates from Satan,
                         is sustained by demonic influence,
                         is often promoted as a joke.

The twisting of the tongue of man leads to convoluted thought,
                         to confusion of My children,
                         to the misleading of The Lambs of God.

The twisting of the tongue of man is a charge laid in anger by his spirit,
                         is the lips spread in successions of his sinning utterances,
                         is that birthed from an intent of evil to deceive his fellow man.

The twisting of the tongue of man has no excuse acceptable to God,
                         has no reason to create such to be a plague on his eternity,
                         has no method of redemption other than appeal.

The twisting of the tongue of man surfaces when momentary control is lost to demons,
                         when silence is filled with that which is allowed to escape,
                         when pride is to the fore to preen a presentation.

The twisting of the tongue of man follows imagined achievements
     spoken to enhance an insignificance,
     spoken to defraud another soul,
     spoken to entice interest in the worthless,
     spoken to make grandiose that which has no value,
     spoken to achieve the sale built on false pretences,
     spoken to establish a relationship with no substance in the statements,
     spoken before a bench to escape accountability from the courts of man,
     spoken in stupidity in the repeating of the hearsay which stands but for a moment:
                         before the crumbling from the lacking of foundations.

The twisting of the tongue of man leads him to his destiny of promise,
                         leads him to a place where he can consider well his actions,
                         leads him into darkness where the light no longer even flickers.

The twisting of the tongue of man carries sin into the grave,
                         outweighs the scales of his endeavours,
                         tips the scales of honour,
                         destroys the scales of righteousness,
                         bemuses the scales of truth,
                         weighs down the scales of sin,

>   blindfolds the scales of justice,
>   vacates the scales of God.

The twisting of the tongue of man
> surfaces to placate when silence is the course of wisdom,
> surfaces to mislead away from a time of shame,
> surfaces in an attempt to exonerate from what was wilful and deliberate,
> surfaces as exaggeration rules both the soul and the lips,
> surfaces in denial when an apology is called for,
> surfaces in hate from lips well impregnated with honey,
> surfaces in misplaced love when the truth is judged as too much to bear.

The twisting of the tongue of man was a gift from Satan in the garden,
>> from the serpent with disaster,
>> from the herding of the fallen angels.

The twisting of the tongue of man is readily perceived by God,
> is readily the decider of a journey,
> is readily the loser of all the promises but one.

The twisting of the tongue of man has no recourse in eternity,
> has no recourse to a testimony,
> has no recourse to the blood.

The twisting of the tongue of man only has the recourse of falling in the quest for mercy
>   at the bema."

My Content Study Aid

_____
_____
_____
_____
_____
_____
_____
_____
_____
_____
_____
_____
_____

The Sealing of The Temple

"The sealing of the temple confirms progression of the soul,
        follows the polishing of the soul,
        achieves a milestone for the spirit of man,
        grants access to the altar where high service is required within
                                The Fear of God.

The sealing of the temple affirms The Will of God,
        imposes the stamp of God upon a life,
        enlarges access when in audience with God.

The sealing of the temple shows the glow of lampstands all in use,
        shows an open door for access to The Living Water,
        shows the way to the hard won victory at The Cross.

The sealing of the temple inaugurates and withstands,
        secures and upholds,
        enables and accomplishes.

The sealing of the temple bespeaks the ways of God, bespeaks
        the desires of God, bespeaks the
        companionship of God.

The sealing of the temple has assurance within the fold of God,
        expresses His Will within His wisdom,
        projects the life within His care.

The seal upon the temple is The Kiss of God,
        is the handprint of The Lord,
        is the signing of My Spirit.

The seal within the temple denotes purity on record,
        denotes the soul under control,
        denotes the confidence of God.

The seal withheld from a temple speaks of a work in progress,
        speaks of a work without the due priority,
        speaks of a work meandering on its way.

The seal withheld from a temple sees assumptions in existence
        which may prove to be invalid,
        which may fail before improvements are completed,
        which do not meet the understandings of the cross.

The seal withheld from a temple should be keenly sought,
        should be keen for a reappraisal,
        should be keen to see the tasks polished and presented,

assessed and corrected,
inspected and verified for truth.
The seal withheld from a temple should have the blemishes removed,
the tarnishing repolished,
the soiling treated with the bleach,
the ramparts fortified for the defence,
the dungeons cleared of the debris:
should signpost the ownership of God."

My Content Study Aid

The Compulsion of The Soul

"The compulsion of the soul is in the presence of an agency exerting delegated force,
                of an agency of domination,
                of an agency neither respecting nor
                        honouring the freewill of man.

The compulsion of the soul has made an outlaw of the spirit,
        has thrown the spirit to the wolves,
        has adopted another entity to follow into subservience.

The compulsion of the soul started with a flavour,
        moved into an urging,
        settled in a habit,
        was in a game of tag,
        graduated to fighting in a battle,
        became lost and defeated in a war.

The compulsion of the soul pays tribute by the captured,
        pays a heavy rental for what was once seen as his,
        pays homage as a captive to that once thought as both benign and helpful.

The compulsion of the soul denies access to retreat,
        access to return to the way once known,
        access to the locked and barred:
        access to the gate to freedom which a prisoner cannot reach.

The compulsion of the soul is logged and bound,
        is victimised and unfriendly,
        is dishonest and untruthful.

The compulsion of the soul shouts and bullies,
        scares and frustrates,
        grabs and swallows.

The compulsion of the soul holds a needle in reserve, holds
        the cash in readiness, holds the
        backstop out of sight.

The compulsion of the soul has no compassion for the body;
        treats the body as a slave;
        sees no semblance in the body's being;
        takes the body down a road of torture—
                where the body becomes a former shadow of itself.

The compulsion of the soul is immune to love,
        to care,
        to pleading.

The compulsion of the soul is as self-centred as a whirlwind,
        is as friendly as a viper,
        is as forgiving as the pay dirt needed for another deal.
The compulsion of the soul results in its subversiveness in dealings,
        continues until it reaches the far boundaries of distraught despair,
        needs to hear a testimony of one released from subterfuge,
        needs to grasp the possibility of redemption,
        needs to become committed to a life when filed for another destiny.
The compulsion of the soul can be overcome,
        can be surmounted,
        can be vanquished with the cause.
The compulsion of the soul can become a term relegated to the past,
        can become a term forsaken and despised,
        can become a term with the practicality of a promise for new life.
The compulsion of the soul can be changed into a blessing;
        can join the franchise of God;
        can walk in His discipleship and know wonders in the soul;
        can get to know the spirit and to rejoice together at the changes."

My Content Study Aid

_____
_____
_____
_____
_____
_____
_____
_____
_____
_____
_____
_____
_____
_____

The Non-vindictiveness of God

"God is not vindictive in His rebuking of man.

God is not vindictive when the record of the miscreant is found to be imperfect
>> on which the judgment may appear to rest:
>> on which the judgment may be incurred,
>> on which the judgment may be sought,
>> on which the judgment is likely to be proclaimed.

God is not vindictive when warnings of behaviour have been issued,
> even when the accountability for such behaviour has been declared,
> even when the penalties for infringement have been written down and sealed as the word of God,
> even when the basis of redemption is both wilfully and patently ignored,
> even when the warnings for encouraging compliance are treated with nothing but contempt.

Man does not deserve and never will deserve vindictiveness—
>> the planning for revenge—
>> not held as present as a desire of God.

God is not a seeker of revenge,
>> leaves it within the domain of man.

God is the imposer of His vengeance reserved solely unto Himself:
>>> that which God insists is not shareable by man;
>>> that which God states should never be usurped by man.

The vengeance of God manifests with the occasioned falling of His wrath,
>> manifests as timed by His prophets whom He knows,
>> manifests as bound within His promises affecting man.

Vengeance with the wrath of God are awe full to behold;
>> are terrifying to be under:
>> leave very few survivors among those repudiating God."

My Content Study Aid

_____
_____
_____
_____
_____

The Sacrifice of Self

"Sacrifice of self is the sparking of discipleship,
        is the confirmation of the setting of a goal,
        is the freewill of man being self-limiting on an aspect of his life.

Sacrifice of self is as a mushroom cloud exploding,
        reaches to the heights,
        expands into the distance,
        surveys a great expanse readied for rebuilding.

Sacrifice of self modifies behaviour,
        modifies the input to the body soul and spirit,
        modifies the output from the body soul and spirit.

Sacrifice of self introduces concern for others,
        offers help in need,
        shares The Building Blocks of Faith.

Sacrifice of self deserts the cause of shame,
        deserts the cause of blemishes upon a gown,
        deserts the need to place a muzzle on a mouth,
        deserts the actions leading to the binding of the hands and feet of man,
        deserts the shallowness of existence for a life with purpose and results.

Sacrifice of self trusts and believes,
        offers and adjusts,
        discusses and acquires:
                the offerings of God.

Sacrifice of self learns and emulates,
        masters and decides,
        appraises and discards:
                along the road of discipleship.

Sacrifice of self verifies and adopts,
        seeks and finds,
        is both blessed and favoured:
                as wisdom is acquired.

Sacrifice of self removes the mountain tops for a surveyor's peg,
        removes the mountain of discrimination,
        shares the mountain of testimonies,
        guards The Mountain of Faith as it grows from deep within.

Sacrifice of self sees the mountain of salvation for what it really is,
        when the striving fails to yield reward:
                a molehill as in a garden,

> a mound upon the river's bank wherein The Living Water Flows—
> surrounded by Much Grace—
> lying there to be but picked up and donned.

Sacrifice of self is not a trite expression in the vocabulary of man,
> is not diminished by much use.

Sacrifice of self is a sacred trust,
> opens the path to holiness,
> stems the tide of debris,
> casts no shadow in The Son's Light.

Sacrifice of self ends the conflicts of the soul,
> knows the approach of harmony,
> has eyes which can now see the lands beyond horizons.

Sacrifice of self is not a death sentence on the body,
> is not dressed in mourning,
> is not bedecked with tears of regret,
> is not starved of input.

Sacrifice of self brings a new sun rise to each day,
> brings a new prayer upon the lips,
> brings a new exchange in the relationship with God.

Sacrifice of self majors in the perpetual,
> graduates to the eternal,
> swaps the disasters of the past for the promises within the present,
> > for a way of life unveiled,
> > for success concluded within the guidelines of The Spirit,
> > > for the golden goal of God."

My Content Study Aid

_____
_____
_____
_____
_____
_____
_____
_____
_____

The Grain of Wood

"The grain of wood testifies of Me,
    in its layering and its patterning,
    in its softness and its hardness,
    in its pliability and its stiffness,
    in its moulding and its resistance,
    in its growth rings of proximity,
    in its homeland where it flourishes,
    in its colour and its adornment:
        as fitted for the chosen use of man.

The grain of wood is a marvel as presented unto man.

The grain of wood is shaped and bent,
    is steamed and soaked,
    is dried and weathered:
        in conforming with the will of man.

The grain of wood receives surface impregnations to enhance and to preserve,
        to beautify and to astonish,
        to attract and trade in acquisition.

The grain of wood supports and comforts man.

The grain of wood renews and multiples,
    warms and heats,
    shelters and protects:
        the shelters built for man.

The grain of wood is present in all aspects of the life of man.

The grain of wood is valued and sought after,
    is tested and rejected,
    is appraised and accepted:
      meets with man's wastage in destruction when judged as in the way.

The grain of wood serves man along his timeline of progression.

The grain of wood partakes in the birthplaces of the forests,
    partakes in the birthplaces of the breath of man,
    partakes in the extending of renewal to the birds within the sky;
        to the animals upon The Earth;
        to the animals and fish within the seas:
    all in need of covering and breath under the dominion of man."

The Stones of The Earth

"The stones of The Earth have a value imposed by rarity,
                are discovered and uplifted from The Earth,
                are plain and unused to the eyes of man,
                are manipulated in the hands of man,
                are worked by the hands of man
                              so the inherent beauty is displayed,
                              so the value of the gemstone rises—
                                          as it is magnified and set in gold.

      So the golden setting enhances and enthrals,
                      creates envy and great pride,
                      presents love and a lifelong pledge,
                      stores wealth and memories,
                      is plundered and sold in shadows,
                      is lost as it is left behind.

The stones of The Earth either stagnate or circulate,
          may cause a squabble,
          may become the centre of a fight;
          rarely does peace prevail with the claiming of inheritances,
          rarely does violence ensue as ownership transfers—
                          with the opening of the vaults of wealth,
          rarely do the stones of The Earth bring much happiness to man:
                when the locks are checked with the turning of the keys.

The stones of The Earth travel and stay put,
          have the glory on show,
          have the glory hidden,
          make a statement to the world,
          often dwell in the surroundings of state.

The stones of The Earth can hold the wealth of man,
          can measure the wealth of man,
          can progress along the linked paths of generations.

The stones of The Earth can support a regency,
          can validate a throne,
          can maintain a war.

The stones of The Earth are collected and cut by man;
          are both bonded and free,
          are both loved and hated,
          are both segregated and pooled,
          are both showered and withdrawn,

      are both admitted and denied,
      are both despoiled and enhanced,
      are both honoured and dishonoured in the handling by man.

The spirits of Heaven are each unique and crafted,
      are valued in their being,
      are birthed for uplifting into arms,
      are in a new stage of development as each sees the eyes of man,
      are handled and fondled with great care,
      are clothed and dressed by man as beauty is admired,
          so the value rises with the addition of the soul set within a home.

So the setting of the soul enhances both:
          as they commence a journey locked together in a body,
            with a lifelong pledge of companionship together.

So the soul is subjected to envy and great pride;
    has love misplaced and yearning;
      stores the wealth of wisdom as it is permitted to accumulate within the
            existence of the being of the soul;
      is attacked with the view of conquest;
      is sheltered and protected by the counsel of the spirit which attempts to
            hold its hand;
      is robbed of its integrity as the handhold of instruction is casually
            shrugged off;
      is affirmed and lively as the handhold of the spirit is keenly grasped and
            valued as a link to life.

The spirits of Heaven are tasked by My Spirit,
      are each tasked to supervise their souls,
      are each tasked to lead their appointed soul with guidance
            and direction,
      are each tasked to take the soul upon a journey of introduction,
          upon a journey of resolution,
          upon a journey of integration.

The spirit of man has a struggle set before him,
      has a struggle with his soul of purpose,
      has a struggle to bring to pass The Will of God.

The spirit of man is instated as the captain of his soul,
        to win over the freewill of the soul,
        to bless the soul with care and love,
        to encourage and uplift the soul into the very presence of God.

The spirit of man should not submit to any entity before an altar unless affirmed by God,
        unless it is The Altar of The Lamb,
          unless it beckons with eternal life into The Family of God.

The spirit of man is accountable for the soul of man,
>> to teach and to instruct,
>> to translate and to confirm,
>> to interpret and to consolidate,
>> to persevere and to overcome,
>> to enable and to entrain the soul to follow
>>>> in righteousness and truth.

The spirit of man knows of the second death,
>> that which he is most anxious to avoid,
>> that which marks the freewill failure to concede by the soul
>>>> beset with obstinacy:
>> that which extinguishes all hope and expectation.

For as man lives,
> so will he die.

The soul of man is birthed to have a captain,
>> is birthed to be successful,
>> is birthed to become acquainted with the fellowship of God.

The soul of man struggles against confinement,
>> tussles with the truth,
>> seeks freedom within the will of man,
>> is unacquainted with the concept of freewill,
>>>> of the responsibility,
>>>> of the blessings and the curses,
>>>> of the accountability he stands in need
>>>>> of learning—
>>>> with acceptance of the spirit's goal.

The soul of man stands in need of adopting with commitment the spirit's leading into
>>>> truth and righteousness,
>>>> and the giftings of The Spirit,
>> so they may be a matching pair:
>> so the matching pair are known to God
>>>> and become entrusted to direct the body
>>>> with assuredness of deed and action—
>> so none are put at risk of that from which they cannot arise.

The soul of man can be pulled both to and fro:
>> can become a battleground fraught with indecision,
>> can become a battle ground fed by the pleasures of the soul,
>> can become a battle ground tugged by the spirit into the light of Christ,
>> can become a battle ground for two conflicting targets,
>> can become a battle ground between The God of Eternal Love
>>>> and the devil with his coming anguish,
> can become a battle ground where the freewill of man is hoisted on a stake—

Anthony A Eddy (Scribe)

  a stake binding imprisonment with Satan or,
  a stake holding up the cross of freedom with The Living Lord of Love.

So the wise will comprehend,
so the wise will make connections,
so the wise will receive the message as intended,
so the wise will interpret,
so the wise will speak,
so the wise will listen for the heralds."

My Content Study Aid

The Wind of My Spirit (2)

"The wind of My Spirit is coming as a gale;
        will put man on his knees;
        will put man in his hiding holes:
                before the mighty rushing wind.

The wind of My Spirit gets the attention of man who ponders far too long,
        gets the attention of man who ponders not at all,
        gets the attention of man who ponders on the wonders and
                fully understands.

The wind of My Spirit comes to testify of Me:
        when others were found wanting,
        when others turned aside,
        when others were seen as deaf and dumb,
        when others would not harvest,
        when others would not gather,
    when others would not share the living water from within.

The wind of My Spirit blows around and through,
        blows over and under,
        blows gently and fiercely:
                according to the obstruction,
                according to the rejection,
                according to the recognition.

The wind of My Spirit is scented for the soul,
        is received by the soul in declaration,
                in commitment,
                in discipleship,
        is honoured by the soul in wisdom,
        is taught to the soul in learning,
        is invited to stay by the soul introduced to God.

The wind of My Spirit comes with a sign to man,
        announces His arrival,
        departs without a scene.

The wind of My Spirit can recover and repair the damaged soul of man,
        can oversee and encourage the distraught soul of man,
        can care for and love the lonely soul of man,
        can mitigate and bless the cursed soul of man,
        can adopt and encompass the repentant soul of man.

The wind of My Spirit confirms the heart of godly hope,
        confirms the heart of godly faith,

confirms the heart of godly practice,
confirms the heart of godly seeking,
confirms the heart of godly knowledge,
confirms the heart of godly commitment.

The wind of My Spirit brings the scent of victory,
brings the scent of gardens,
brings the scent of well-being before The Lord.

The wind of My Spirit wafts and wanes,
encircles and transmits,
guards from molestation.

The wind of My Spirit carries Grace before it,
dispenses in like measure of acceptance,
moves on before the tongue can partake in denial.

The wind of My Spirit can impart fire upon the lips ready to proclaim,
can install The Tongues of Heaven,
can test the heart for purity of intent,
can read the character of the soul,
can assess the progress of the spirit.

The wind of My Spirit knows the disease of Satan:
knows its presence and its actions;
knows its miseries of consequences and its landfalls of results;
knows its methods of attack and the evidence resulting.

The wind of My Spirit attends both the godly and the ungodly,
both the righteous and the carnal,
both the sacred and the secular:
that all may come to know their God.

The wind of My Spirit hastens and encourages;
reports and bears witness;
teaches and enhances:
the understanding of the things of God."

Scribal Note: *Refer also to:* 'The Wind of The Spirit' in His 2nd book,
GOD Speaks to Man on the Internet.

My Content Study Aid

_____
_____
_____
_____

The Misery of Man (2)

"The misery of man stems from his pressure to perform,
        stems from his heightened expectations,
        stems from his desire for pampering,
        stems from his thirst for addictive offerings,
        stems from his outlook on his fellow man,
        stems from comparisons of lifestyles so attained.

The misery of man is bred from his despising that which he has gained,
              that which he has achieved,
              that which he compares,
              that which he values,
              that which wastes his years,
              that which brings no satisfaction except on
                          the day of purchase.

The misery of man serves no outlet but self-pity,
        knows no king at home within a residence,
        serves no king within a kingdom,
        visits no king with kingdom living,
        knows not a queen in waiting,
        sees no princes in the wings.

The misery of man is not open to adoption,
        shuts the door on visitors,
        shouts in his frustration,
        ignores the counsel of the wise,
        seeks the solace of the fool,
        drowns his sufferings by seeking the bottoms of a glass.

The misery of man curtails the search for happiness,
        curtails a trip of joy,
        curtails contact within a family,
        curtails the care of self,
        curtails the chatter of the children,
        curtails the laughter in a home.

The misery of man is a child of depression,
        is a child inflicted by an enemy of man,
        is a child never seen in maturity,
        is a child without a smile,
        is a child of envy,
        is a child of pride.

The misery of man is spawned through loss of hope,

        is spawned through loss of vision,
        is spawned through loss of youth,
        is spawned through loss of relationship,
        is spawned through loss of achievement,
        is spawned through loss of freedom.

The misery of man can be observed within his eyes,
        can be gauged from a selfish spirit,
        can be measured by his walk,
        can be assessed from the company he keeps,
        can be determined from the input to his soul,
        can be seen in his attitude to God.

The misery of man stews its own brew of bitterness,
        stews its own brew of complaints,
        stews its own brew of sour staleness,
        stews its own brew to seal the darkness overhead,
        stews its own brew for moping,
        stews its own brew waiting for rancour to surface.

The misery of man turns cabbages into sauerkraut,
        turns potatoes into mash,
        turns dried peas into mush,
        turns sunlight into nightmares,
        turns love into hate,
        turns the enemy of man into his friend.

The misery of man is a disappointment to God,
        clears the thrones of prospective occupants,
        destroys the lineage of kings,
        beggars man to leave the promises incapable of fulfilment,
        places the soul of man beyond the reach of kith and kin,
        blames God for his weighty load of sin,
        listens only to satanic counsel as bound to his freewill.

The misery of man can climb out of his cage,
        can unlock the door of darkness,
            has the key in hand to escape into the sunlight.

The misery of man can turn the trip around,
        can pay attention to the call upon his life,
        can decide to seek and serve.

The misery of man can become the exaltation of man
        in but a moment of understanding,
        in the shedding of the past,
        in the welcoming of a future,
        in the flash of inspiration which opens the pathway to the stars.

The misery of man is not intended to be a gnawing bone for devils,
> is not intended to summit in despair,
> is not intended to be a mark of failure.

The misery of man can be cleansed and polished,
> can become reflective,
> can have the blemishes removed,
> can see the cracks and dents erased,
> can bounce back whole and reinvigorated,
> can sing the song of victory in the presence of The Lamb."

Scribal Note: *Refer to* 'The Misery of Man' *in His third book,*
> *GOD Speaks as His Spirit Empowers.*

My Content Study Aid

The Dependencies of Man

"The dependencies of man make man far from as independent as he would often think:
    fill man with assumptions which may or may not be true;
    travel round in circles with the interlocking of the sphere;
    see familiarity raise levels of contempt;
    have the life stations working hard to preserve the levels of support for man;
    know the onset of the scrambling to maintain the viability of man.

The dependencies of man are many and varied,
    originate for both the short term and the long term of man,
    keep man alive and comfortable upon his home within the firmament of God.

The dependencies of man lie beyond his beck and call,
    lie beyond the reach of his impatient hand,
    lie beyond the effectiveness of his voice of desperation.

The dependencies of man have feedback loops in place:
    have feedback loops of augmentation;
    have feedback loops to prevent wastage from a surplus;
    have feedback loops for continuation;
    have feedback loops assessing errors in the standard deviation;
    have feedback loops under the guiding hand of God.

The dependencies of man care for man beyond his comprehension,
    beyond the existence of his knowledge,
    beyond the application of his time containment.

The dependencies of man overlook man's plighting of his troth,
    overlook the keeping of his word,
    overlook man's fitness for an extended journey of renown.

The dependencies of man reverberate around his homeland,
    reverberate towards the stars,
    reverberate in the lodging place of angels,
    reverberate in the heavens administered by God.

The dependencies of man reverberate with the timing for review,
    reverberate in expectation of the installing of new settings,
    reverberate to call to notice the coming aeon of great change."

The Glory on Man

"The glory on man is an attribute of presence,
        is an attribute transcending jurisdictions:
          is an attribute present in the mortality of man in the company of his spirit;
          is an attribute present in the eternity of man in the company of his spirit.

The glory on man is on his countenance when in the presence of The God of Love,
          as My Spirit leads in worship,
            as The Father attends upon His Throne of Grace.

The glory on man is not starved for affection,
        is not starved by Satan standing on a rock that rocks,
        is not starved when perception is to the fore and the background
                                    is confused.

The glory on man speaks a different language,
        speaks the language of God,
        speaks the language not uttered through the mouth,
        speaks the language for which man is intended,
        speaks the language in which the lips and tongue are both stilled
                                    and stationary.

The glory on man needs his time of preparation to attain fulfilment of experience,
            to obtain fluency of expression,
            to reach the higher level of reality
                      required by a jump from time.

The glory on man is on those who know their God,
        is on The Saints of God,
        is on The Multitudes of God,
        is on The Disciples of The Son,
        is marked as for The Bride.

The glory on man neither oscillates nor fluctuates,
        only intensifies as it reflects,
        only magnifies the pure and the spotless,
        only signs the presence of the willing servants of The Lord.

The glory on man is not seen when looking in a mirror,
        is not there upon enquiry,
        is not to the fore when pride is seen to linger for acceptance.

The glory on man breaks the language barrier imposed on man,
          prepares him for a walk of wonder with instant access and response,
          sets him on the voyage of discovery fully able and familiar
                                    with the language of God.

The glory on man discerns the prepared and the unprepared,
>   those who progress The Tongues of Heaven
>   >   and those who place them in a waiting basket,
>   those crossing into new horizons
>   >   and those settling for the dawn and dusk,
>   those who learn to interpret while they speak
>   >   and those still overcome with the wasting
>   >   >   fear of man.

The glory on man awaits the adventuring of man,
>   awaits the progress in his preparation,
>   awaits the call to hearken and to transmit on the oscillations known to God,
>   awaits the growth in the spirit's knowledge to open the door with access:
>   >   to the multi-way communication of the soul with his waiting God."

My Content Study Aid

Behold The Bride of Christ

"Behold The Three in One coming from the east.

Behold The Father of creation.
Behold The Son of sacrifice.
Behold The Spirit of great magnitude.

Behold The Triumvirate in victory.
Behold The Trifold Partnership of God coming for the stars of man.

Behold the scene of God bringing victory to those engaged at portholes,
                      to those awaiting Son-rise,
                      to those prepared and dressing
                                  for The Wedding of The Lamb.

Behold the sky prepared for launching,
    the sky in all its finery,
    the sky filled with the majesty of might.

Behold the sequence of presentation.
Behold the ripples of decision.

Behold the waves of tears.
Behold the waves of grace.
Behold the waves of fulfilment.

Behold the waves of man.

Behold perfection in its quest.
Behold perfection in its call.
Behold perfection in its rejection.
Behold perfection in its acceptance.
Behold perfection instated on The Earth.
Behold perfection enthroned for all eternity.
Behold perfection in the company of God.

Behold glory raining down.
Behold glory reigning up.
Behold glory intermingled.

Behold glory well bestowed.

Behold the music of endowment.
Behold the music of the fanfares.
Behold the music of progression.

Behold the music of annunciation.
Behold the music of the angels.
Behold the music of the throne room of God.
Behold the music of the heavens.

Behold The Bride of Christ before the sunrise.
Behold The Bride of Christ before the elevation.
Behold The Bride of Christ before the segregation.
Behold The Bride of Christ before the separation.
Behold The Bride of Christ before the establishment of purity.
Behold The Bride of Christ before the vanquishing of the rank and vile.

Behold My Word established.
Behold My Word upheld.
Behold My Word of warning.
Behold My Word of promise.
Behold My Word of strength.
Behold My Word of truth.

Behold My Word of application to My Bride."

My Content Study Aid

My Relationship with Man

"I,
    The Lord,
        speak to My servant Anthony this day,
            that he may act as My scribe in all he hears Me say,
                  in all he hears Me teach,
                  in all he hears Me task.

I,
    The Lord Jesus,
        of the heavens and of The Earth,
            say to man this day within reach of this,
                      My word,
        'Vacate and change your ways less you are smitten by My wrath.

        Vacate and dismiss your habits of a lifetime—
                those which can only lead you downwards.

        Vacate and turn again forsaking your destruction of your fellow man—
                in all its many guises which prevent,
                      which stall,
                      which place stumbling blocks along
            the pathway of his economic progress,
                his ability to achieve fair trades,
                his seeking to be treated righteously:
                      by those he is forced to encounter in his effort
                            for his family to survive.'

I,
    The Lord Jesus,
        say to man this day,
            'The golden rule for man is alive and well within the law of God,
                is capable of recording accountability,
                is the bearer of the injuries imposed,
                is the flag ship of the estate of man,
                is the out-working of the message of relationship,
                is the invader and disposer of the field of sin,
                is the archetype from the teaching of The Cross,
                is the defence in truth for any accusation levelled
                      at the behaviour of a soul.'

I,
    The Lord Jesus,
        say to man this day,
            'Do unto others as you would have them do unto you.'

I,
>The Lord Jesus,
>>say to man this day,
>>>'For as you treat so you shall be treated.
>>>For as you deceive so it shall be meted.
>>>For as you choose the measure so it shall be measured out to you.'

I,
>The Lord Jesus,
>>say to man this day,
>>>'Beware.
>>>Behold.

>>>Those who live by the law shall be judged by the law.
>>>Those who call on the law are subject to the law.
>>>Those who suffer under the law can appeal the judgment of the law of man.'

I,
>The Lord Jesus,
>>say to man this day,
>>>'If you choose the law know well the call for mercy and the mercy seat.
>>>If you choose the law treat it with respect.
>>>If you choose the law abide by its decision.
>>>If you choose the law you are bound by its effect upon your life and upon your family.'

I,
>The Lord Jesus,
>>say to man this day,
>>>'Beware the law which has been superseded in the interests of man.
>>>Beware of the law which man will fail to keep.
>>>Beware of the law which man does not remember.
>>>Beware of the law of which man stands in ignorance.
>>>Beware of the law which does not shed a tear.
>>>Beware of the law for governing The Multitude of man.'

I,
>The Lord Jesus,
>>say to man this day,
>>>'Behold the free fall of Grace.
>>>Behold how Grace settles.
>>>Behold how Grace wets and thaws.

>>>Behold how Grace can break the chains of imprisonment,
>>>>can break the yoke of enslavement,

        can lighten and remove the burdens,
        can move the mountains around which man walks
                      in circles.

Behold Grace's ease of access.
Behold Grace's ease of acceptance.
Behold Grace's manifold bearing on a life.

Behold My offer placed before the face of man that frees him from the law,
        that offers a promise he cannot redeem himself,
        that grants the promise he's been seeking with
                a new covenant in place.'

I,
   The Lord Jesus,
      say to man this day,
          'Accept and receive the offer of My Grace from The Loving God.
      Endow your generations with the gifts of The Living God.

      Seek The Truth in action.
      Seek The Truth in being.
      Seek The Truth which is everlasting.

      Seek The Truth within the light of Grace:
              for a new beginning with The God of action,
              for a new beginning of My relationship with you.' "

My Content Study Aid

_____
_____
_____
_____
_____
_____
_____
_____
_____
_____
_____
_____

The Washing of The Clothes

"The washing of the clothes brings woman to the well,
                brings woman to the riverbank,
                brings woman to the slapping stone,
                brings woman to the scrubbing board,
                brings woman to the wash house,
                brings woman to the laundry,
                brings woman to the clothes line,
                brings woman to the drying area,
                brings woman to the iron,
                brings woman to the folded shelf of man.

The washing of the clothes removes the stains and spots,
                removes the dirt and sweat of yesterday,
                removes the odours and the scents ingrained upon the cloth.

The washing of the clothes has keen eyes on inspection,
                views the rents and tears,
                views the runs and catches,
                views the holes and spills.

The washing of the clothes notes the missing and the worn,
                notes the need for darning,
                notes the need for buttons,
                notes the need for repairing the ravages of thorns,
                notes the need for a larger size,
                notes the call for a replacement as the old outlive the function
                              of the purpose.

The washing of the clothes does not wash the body soul or spirit:
                leaves the blemishes intact,
                displays the stains on view,
                covers up the muck of yesterday—
                              pretends it never happened.

The washing of the clothes presents a shabby body as in a covering of care,
                as in a covering prepared for the dressage of the soul,
                as in a covering hiding the shame beneath,
                as in a covering designed to mask the body soul and spirit
                        from an ineffectual assessment of their well-being.

The washing of the clothes presents a covering fully suited to a temple receiving little or
                                                            no attention.

The washing of the clothes does not mask the status of The Temple from the eyes of God.

The washing of the clothes should follow the cleansing of the house,

　　　　　　　　　　the inspection of the premises,
　　　　　　　　　　the conversion to A Temple.

The washing of the clothes does not hide the potential of a temple, does
　　　　　　　　not close the thoroughfares of Satan, does not
　　　　　　　　preclude the trampling of the hordes
　　　　　　　　　　　　　　through the corridors of power,
　　　　　　　　does not exclude the rooms of darkness yet to see the light,
　　　　　　　　does not mend the broken fence yet to see the hand
　　　　　　　　　　　　　　　　of the carpenter in action.

The washing of the clothes does not bestow immunity from filth within The Temple:
　　　　　　　　　　　　from surfacing in times of stress,
　　　　　　　　　　　　from appearing in a time of anger
　　　　　　　　　　　　　when The Temple Shakes.

The washing of the clothes brings sparkle and a sheen befitting of A Temple
　　　　　　　when The Temple is cleansed and washed,
　　　　　　　　　　is honour bound in purity of intent,
　　　　　　　　　　is circumcised and ready with its armour
　　　　　　　　　　　　　for the attacks of Satan.

The washing of the clothes is not of great importance to God,
　　　　　　　can have the importance misconstrued by man,
　　　　　　　is without significance to My Spirit's being,
　　　　　　　is an adjunct to the body found necessary by man,
　　　　　　　is an appeal to fancy and to decoration,
　　　　　　　is an appeal to comfort and to implication,
　　　　　　　is an appeal to status and to inheritance of man.

The washing of the clothes imparts understanding of the reason for the presentation:
　　　　　　　when the hanger still stands in need,
　　　　　　　when the wardrobe is still filled with insects of destruction,
　　　　　　　when the pathway to the drying clothes is still composed
　　　　　　　　　　　　　of stumbling blocks."

My Content Study Aid

_____
_____
_____
_____
_____
_____

The Game Hunters of The Earth

"The game hunters of The Earth are a selfish breed apart,
                have no vision for the future,
                are the strippers of the scenes,
                are the bereft of thought and reason,
                are not amiss to poaching a sought prize,
                are not concerned with consequences,
                are the targeters of the scarce and threatened,
                are the bit takers seeking profit,
                leave the profitless to the scavengers,
                discard the mutilated to the fastest predator.

The game hunters of The Earth cover the air,
                the land,
                the sea,
                the ice,
                the snow in a quest of pride,
                          in a quest for profit,
                          in a quest for self-aggrandisement,
                          in a quest for satisfaction of the self:
    which sees the carcass left in the rear to rot,
    which sees the carcass butchered where it fell,
    which sees the carcass presented before the market place of man—
                destined as a plate of luxury,
                as a curiosity exhibited in cages,
                as a beast upon a leash where compassion is non-existent.

The game hunters of The Earth leave the orphans to their fate:
                leave the orphans without asylum;
                leave the orphans without reserve;
                leave the orphans without value;
                leave theorphans without recourse,
                leave the orphans without protection.

The game hunters of The Earth create orphans without excuse.
The game hunters of The Earth rape and pillage that for which they do not care.
The game hunters of The Earth shout and cheer at each lop-sided victory ending
                                                              in defeat.

The game hunters of The Earth know the shot and whistle,
                know the bow and arrow,
                know the ship and net,
                know the mother ship and calf,
                know the rod and line,

                know the dog and knife,
                know the bird and glove,
                know the spear and club,
                know the bird with blades and refuge in the wilderness.

The game hunters of The Earth put no constraints on limit,
                are a law unto themselves,
                are vigorous in their pursuit,
                offer no means of escape,
                pursue a quarry unto death.

The game hunters of The Earth have a history of ignominy,
                have a history of waste,
                have a history of greed,
                have a history of disgrace,
                have a history of overkill,
                have a history of non-respect.

The game hunters of The Earth do not limit in preservation,
                    will continue unto extinction,
                    will watch and wait for the very last.

The game hunters of The Earth have misapplied the charter of dominion,
                    have misapplied the scape goat of the cull,
                    have misapplied the excuse of research.

The game hunters of The Earth search for the escape clause,
                twist the meaning of intent,
                penetrate the boundaries of exclusion,
                breach the limits on a catch,
                take all they can get,
                are not concerned with life,
                buy their way into the garnering of votes.

The game hunters of The Earth are summoned within a replevin—
                      both for their pickings and for being afoul
                                    of the intent of God."

My Content Study Aid

_____

_____

_____

_____

_____

The Magnificence of God

"The magnificence of God is worth the waiting to encounter,
        is worth the effort of man to establish his relationship,
        is worth the surrendering of the gold of God as held by man,
        is worth the time of man in preparation,
        is worth the obedience to the tasking of My Spirit,
        is worth the thankful heart for the gift of Grace.

The magnificence of God has perfection in accoutrements,
        has perfection in surroundings,
        has perfection in The Family of God.

The magnificence of God cannot be presented in fullness before man in his mortality,
        cannot be adequately described in a vocabulary where such
                words lack existence,
        cannot be envisioned as to scope and portrayal when eternity
                has no depth of meaning,
        cannot be submitted to the worthy
            when their eyes are not renewed,
            when the veil of protection is still essential to be in place,
            when the concept of dimensions still leaves queries in the
                spirits and the souls.

So active Faith is to the fore in this,
        the time of man,
        to deal with things which yet remain unseen:
            while the time for open declaration—
                of the access of intimacy—
            is still awaited by The Bride in preparation,
                by the angels with excitement.

The magnificence of God furnishes the heavens and all so contained therein,
        furnishes The Earth and all so contained thereon.

The magnificence of God is to be viewable by man—
            the miniatures in the microcosm,
            the gargantuas in the macrocosm.

The magnificence of God has an earthly representation in His Edifice as built by man,
        has a heavenly existence in His Edifice as built by God.

The magnificence of God is not an idle speculation,
        is not foreseeing the unforeseeable,
        is not proposing the imagining of a fallacy,
        is not portraying a non-existence.

The magnificence of God is in touch with reality,
                is in touch with The Spirit,
                is in touch with the gifts,
                is in touch with His desire for the welfare of man.

The magnificence of God enthuses man even unto death,
                even unto the blessing of the new covenant of exploration,
                even unto the be all and the end all of creation,
                even unto the wonders of the environment of man.

The magnificence of God has established without peer:
                has optioned the destiny of man while preserving his freewill,
                has filled His world with Grace for man just by his asking,
                has reconciled man unto his God—
                          with the redemption of man's spirit soul and body.

The magnificence of God fulfils His magnificence of character,
                His magnificence of steadfastness,
                His magnificence of being,
                His magnificence of presence,
                His magnificence of loving,
                His magnificence of relationship,
                His magnificence of integrity.

The magnificence of God fulfils His magnificence of grace,
                His magnificence of glory,
                His magnificence of magnanimity,
                His magnificence of equanimity,
                His magnificence of eternity,
                His magnificence of the progression of man,
                His magnificence of creation.

The magnificence of God fulfils His magnificence of the freewill of man,
                His magnificence of the being of man,
                His magnificence of His patience,
                His magnificence of His word,
                His magnificence of wisdom,
                His magnificence of sharing,
                His magnificence of bestowal.

The magnificence of God is in The Communion with God,
                is in The Trinity of God,
                is in The Temples of God,
                is in The Sacrifice of God,
                is in His Church abounding,
                is in His Fare on offer."

The Voice of Man

"The voice of man is a wonder to behold in its means of production,
                    in its support of clarity,
                    in its response to frequency.

The voice of man has linkage to his ears,
              to become the triplet entwined in functionality,
              to become the impartation of the senses enabling man
                                  to converse at ease.

The voice of man has overtones of uniqueness,
            has qualities of differentiation between the genders,
                        between growth and maturity,
                        between the languages of man,
                        between a whisper and a roar.

The voice of man speaks the will of man,
            speaks the will of demons,
            speaks The Will of God.

The voice of man can get him into trouble,
            can get him out of trouble.

The voice of man can be involved with lies,
            can be the signpost of the truth.

The voice of man can signal and commit,
            can plead and threaten,
            can beg and dominate.

The voice of man can be The Call to God or a weapon of disaster.
The voice of man can utter the cry of terror or the offering of help.

The voice of man has numerous capabilities to adjust unto the moment,
                            to match emotions in an instant,
                            to marry need with the vocality,
                            to equate the circumstances to the
                                          expressions of the soul,
                            to profess the yearning of the spirit.

The voice of man yields to rest,
            yields to the interpretation of the ears,
            yields to the image of the eyes,
            yields to the power of music,
            yields in consent to the voice of God.

The voice of man is amplified and distorted,

    is carried and despatched,
    is packaged and delivered.

The voice of man is recorded as a culprit,
    is recorded as a witness,
    is recorded as an example,
    is recorded as a teacher,
    is recorded for enjoyment,
    is recorded as a record of the past of man.

The voice of man trembles with emotion,
    trembles with rage,
    trembles with age,
    trembles with sickness,
    trembles with compassion.

The voice of man can seek and find,
    can comfort and console,
    can sing the song of joy and the song of mourning.

The voice of man is close to the voice of God,
    is close to The Tongues of Heaven,
    is close to the confirmation of the purpose for a life,
    is close to the measuring of commitment.

The voice of man contains power and authority,
     blasphemy and blessing,
     disdain and adulation.

The voice of man surfaces in wonder and disparagement,
      in worship and profanity,
      in glory and in shame.

Wise is he who knows the approval of God upon his Life,
    the gift of God upon his Tongue,
    the purity of God upon his Voice:
        for such as they are aware of The Fear of God."

My Content Study Aid

_____

_____

_____

_____

_____

The Joy of The Lord

"The joy of The Lord is for The Accompanying of man,
        is The Gift of declaration,
        is The Encourager of companionship,
        is The Happiness of the soul,
        is The Rejoicing of the spirit,
        is The Glow of Glory which attracts the soul in anguish.

The joy of The Lord is concentrated in His Bride-in-Waiting,
        is dispensed from a joy filled heart,
        is handed on by contact built on understanding,
        is present in excess upon the body soul and spirit within the unity
                                  of God.

The joy of The Lord is developed upon reflection of the peace of God,
        is developed within a field of gratitude,
        is developed in a close relationship with God.

The joy of The Lord repels the attacking of demons in concert,
        repels the efforts of yesterday lingering to subdue,
        chases forward out of influence that expected on the morrow.

The joy of The Lord is dwelt in with delight,
        rests within a safe harbour where storms cannot penetrate,
        is for attracting moths unto a searchlight of the night,
        is for attracting sparrows unto the bread laid for the day.

The joy of The Lord broadcasts to the world,
        broadcasts a different way of life:
        broadcasts the love of God unto a hungry world at large,
        broadcasts the presence of My Spirit with the guidance of the feet,
        broadcasts the readiness of The Tongue with the message
                              from The Throne of Grace,
        broadcasts the willingness of God to extend a helping hand,
        broadcasts the presence of The Living Water of which others stand
                                  in need.

The joy of The Lord has no call of fragmentation,
        has no call of disunity,
        has no call of pride,
        has no call of deception,
        honours only truth with love.

The joy of The Lord does not carry chaperones,
        knows well The Holy Spirit from the presence of the thrones.

The joy of The Lord confesses and testifies,
> is always on the lips,
> is readied for divine appointments,
> has access to the answers for the questions of the day.

The joy of The Lord dwells in the field of grace next to the field of love,
> plays in the paddock of relationships where the boundaries
>> are constricted,
> jumps the fence of trials to investigate the field of mountains
>> filled with the weary travellers,
> encourages escape into the paddock where relationships are sound:
>> are reliable,
>> have integrity,
>> are taught to all who choose to enter.

The joy of The Lord puts a skip into a step,
> puts a song upon the lips,
> puts a hug into the arms,
> puts a smile upon a face,
> puts a gift into a hand,
> puts God before a guest,
> puts The Spirit to the fore.

The joy of The Lord is in the blessing of My Spirit,
> is in the favour of The Lord,
> is in the hugging of The Father,
> is in the walk between the thrones,
> is in the presence of the angels who love to be in time."

My Content Study Aid

_____
_____
_____
_____
_____
_____
_____
_____
_____
_____

The Vanguard of My Spirit

"The vanguard of My Spirit is the ideal place for My Saints to be.

For there are the healings and the miracles,
        are the heartaches and the miseries,
        are the testimonies borne,
        are the prayers bestowed with answers,
        are the gifts of My Spirit alive and well within My Saints committed
                            to obedience and blessings.

For there is the forefront of faith in action.

For there is the sprouting of the seed of faith within the witnesses from The Multitudes.

For from there are the testimonies spread—
        like unto the wild fire—
                which proceed the wildfire of My Spirit's presence.

The wildfire of God does not scorch or burn the flesh of man.
The wildfire of God is a sign of wonder as it skips and dances on a journey of delight.

The wildfire of God is not tamed by man,
        is at the behest of God,
        departs and jumps within His will,
        lingers and amazes within the sight of man,
        is an end-time sign to the end-time seekers,
                to the end-time servants of The Living God.

The fire of ashes is not the fire of God,
        is the fire of man—
        can damage and destroy,
        can choke and kill the children of My harvest.

The wildfire of God saves and rescues man,
        uplifts and glorifies The Living God who is ministering
                          in this end-time to His children.

The wildfire of My Spirit is mighty to behold,
        tests the eyes of man to follow,
        tests the body of man to withstand its presence borne of
                          The Fear of God.

The wildfire of God is the flame of My Spirit released from containment in the heavens:
        as a sign to man of My Spirit's being in the domain of man.

For as holiness increases so is felt The Kiss of God upon the body of man
                                    and of His Servants.

For as the fire of God spreads so miracles are encountered,
        so miracles dominate the speech and thoughts of man,
        so miracles defy the explanation
            of those acquainted with their idols,
            of those immersed within a lifestyle of idolatry,
            of those who are familiar with the gods
                who never bring the fire.

My servants know the wonder of discernment,
    know the answers to questions never asked,
    know the history of a family,
        of relationships,
        of sickness and of wasting,
        of the activity of demons,
    with assuredness and certainty.

My servants of The Living God know His servants
            are not left devoid of words upon their lips,
            are not left in silence when a blessing is required,
            are not left in pondering when a rebuke is due.

My servants are not surprised when familiar with the power and the authority of God,
    are not concerned with injury of those receiving ministry,
    are not dismayed by fire in the presence of their God.

My servants are attune with the methodology of impartation through My Spirit,
    have expectations of the truth,
    have the knowledge needed for My ministry as servants of their God.

My servants keep in honour their freewill within their tasking,
    keep in honour their tongue assigned the words of God,
    keep in honour their spirit and their soul in execution of the will of God,
    keep in honour the speaking of the declarations brought by grace,
    keep in honour the relationship built on faith in God,
    keep in honour the miracles rendered as My servants offer up the prayers
        upon their lips in the presence of My Spirit."

My Content Study Aid

_____
_____
_____
_____
_____

The Firestorm of My Spirit

"The firestorm of My Spirit spreads throughout The Earth,
        encounters My Servants with their Faith,
        encounters The Multitudes in their numbers transfixed
              with fear and lack of comprehension,
        encounters the creatures of The Earth with puzzlement
              and wariness.

The firestorm of My Spirit is a sovereign act of God,
        is the visitation of mankind,
        is the testing for Any and Every Sign of Faith
              present on The Earth,
        is a busy time for angels marking up their slates
              with those deciding to seek grace,
        is a time of terror for those with a destiny of default.

The firestorm of My Spirit is not fuelled by alcohol,
        is not fuelled by combustion of a source,
        is not fuelled by the weather at its driest,
        is not fuelled by brush fires lit by man,
        is not fuelled by the works of Satan.

The firestorm of My Spirit is fuelled by The Will of God:
        is fuelled by The Activity of My Spirit,
        is fuelled by The Consent of The Father,
        is fuelled within The Oversight of The Son.

The firestorm of My Spirit ravages and fuses,
        purifies and melds,
        melts and circumcises:
              the hearts and souls of man.

The firestorm of My Spirit travels at amazing speed,
        travels with the sunrise,
        travels unto completion at the sunset.

The firestorm of My Spirit brings The Wrath of God down upon The Earth.

The firestorm of My Spirit leaves no stone unturned where man may hide,
        leaves no cabin of security with immunity,
        leaves no repudiator in the flesh untouched and passed over,
        leaves no sanctuary of man intact and untested.

The firestorm of My Spirit changes the makeup of The Multitudes,
        prepares them for a new beginning,
        removes the dross of man standing in denial,

>   hiding with his fear,
>   brandishing his weapons,
>   protecting his gold,
>   beseeching his idols,
>   chasing after shadows.

The firestorm of My Spirit is seen Quartering The Earth,
>   is seen Riding The Red Horse,
>   is seen assailing the strongholds of Satan,
>   is seen vanquishing his followers,
>   is seen accomplishing the cleansing of The Earth
>   of those bowing in fealty before the prince of darkness.

The firestorm of My Spirit is as a flash of lightning targeting the sin;
>   is as the rumble of the heavens quieting an insurrection—
>   the breakouts of rebellion—
>   the poisoning of the souls;
>   is as the hand of God checking imperfections;
>   is as The Spirit of God Sifting and Verifying The Faithful
>   and the faithless.

The firestorm of My Spirit fights The Battles of My Spirit:
>   fights at Armageddon,
>   fights in the valley of Megiddon,
>   fights where sin is rampant,
>   fights where sin has been unyoked,
>   fights where sin is manifesting to the detriment of My saints."

My Content Study Aid

_____
_____
_____
_____
_____
_____
_____
_____
_____
_____

The Template for The Future

"The template for the future is a document which looks into the future of man in detail—
with the purpose of disclosure.

The template for the future emphasizes the importance of his turning points in life,
    of his actions within his freewill agency,
    of his invited companionship with God,
    of his selecting a destiny worthy of man,
    of his becoming of age in the practising of the gifts of God,
    of his need for attaining fluency in the tongues of My Spirit,
    of his sealing a permanent relationship with God
              as introduced upon the cross of Jesus.

The template for the future portrays a lifestyle for The Stars of God,
    portrays a lifestyle for the friends of Satan:
      for there are neither fence sitters in the garden of God who know not faith,
        nor toe warmers in Hell who do not first test the temperature.

The template for the future is where commitment is ascribed to one and all
        as each heart dictates,
           as actions have so sought to stand in confirmation,
              creating the decrees of intent—
                  the yardsticks of the soul.

The template for the future reads the yardsticks of the soul of man,
      watches the progression one way or the other,
      ensures the integrity of the record so written
                  in the service of eternity.

The template for the future is driven by The Freewill Agency of man,
      does not miss a step in either direction,
      neither restores nor erases without an angel being present.

The template for the future validates the past when called to present the future
                as the present,
      validates the present as the future within each new
            environment where man shall be and is.

The template for the future qualifies and enhances,
      quantifies and discards,
      transfers very quickly in line with the decision,
      sequesters those who have not sought and chosen to ignore,
      liberates those prepared to fly and to so truly soar.

The template for the future cannot be adjusted in the absence of time,
      is determined in the presence of Grace,

has ramifications stretching into eternity.

The template for the future knows the time of preparation,
    knows the time of evaluation,
    knows the time of synchronization,
    knows the time of repudiation,
    knows the time of declaration,
    knows the time of temptation,
    knows the time of acceleration.

The template for the future knows more than man thinks,
    is fully conversant with all within the mantle,
    is satisfied of the sufficiency for the day,
    is primed to handle all which is encountered,
    is confident that justice will prevail,
        that replevins will be addressed,
        that the appeals of man when in mortality will be
                resolved in truth.

The template for the future speaks of the activities of God,
    of the judgement of man,
    of an evaluation resulting in distress,
    of fulfilment of a promise of inheritance with
               happiness to the fore,
    of being in the presence of God,
    of being in the absence of God,
    of the being of man decided by his Own Freewill."

My Content Study Aid

The Home of Godly Wisdom

"The home of Godly wisdom is a sanctuary of love,
    a sanctuary of contentment,
    a sanctuary of happiness with life,
    a sanctuary of well-being with God.

The home of Godly wisdom declares the spirit's unity with the soul,
    declares leadership into eternity,
    declares awareness of My Spirit's Temples,
    declares adoption into the family of God.

The home of Godly wisdom knows the provisioning of God,
    knows the gifts of God,
    knows the taskings of God,
    knows the blessings of God,
    knows the favour of The Lord through a spirit
        sensitized and sensitive to God.

The home of Godly wisdom is welcoming and friendly,
    is solicitous and caring,
    is consolidated and complete.

The home of Godly wisdom is grateful and appreciative,
    is accepting and offering,
    is inspiring and intuitive.

The home of Godly wisdom reflexes and abounds,
    condenses and concentrates,
    approaches and invites.

The home of Godly wisdom has a vestibule of welcome,
    has a vestibule of light,
    has a vestibule where darkness never hides.

The home of Godly wisdom is comfortable and at rest,
    hearkens to the songs of The Spirit,
    has eyes focussed on the vision of the goal.

The home of Godly wisdom has no secrets within its walls,
    has no lies within its eaves,
    has no reflections of shame seen upon its mirrors.

The home of Godly wisdom is an outpost of The Kingdom,
    is an outpost of A Beacon Shining in The Night,
    is an outpost filled with the testimony of The Lord.

The home of Godly wisdom is the sacred amongst the secular,

        is the island lit for standing out,
        is The Lighthouse Flashing Messages to The Multitudes
                                          at large,
        is the refuge set for reclamation,
        is the first aid post equipped and ready for demand,
        is the centre of compassion authorised to dispense
                                 the healing balm of Gilead.

The home of Godly wisdom sees to the warrants of fitness issued
                          for each body soul and spirit:
                          for the underwriter to a journey—
        as each nears completion in the time of preparation.

The home of Godly wisdom is ascribed to the beneficence of God,
        is ascribed to the counsel of The Spirit,
        is ascribed to the construction of a temple,
        is ascribed to a new covenant in place,
        is ascribed to the sacrifice of a father,
        is ascribed to the obedience of a son,
        is ascribed to The Will of The Loving God."

My Content Study Aid

The Wool of My Sheep

"The wool of My sheep is varied both in its texture and its retention of warmth,
        is varied both in its colours and its quality,
        is varied both in its feel and touch,
        is varied both in its length and appearance,
        is varied both in its functioning and its weatherproofing,
        is varied both in locations and environments.

The wool of My sheep portrays a way of life,
        portrays the care of the shepherd,
        portrays the care of the sheep.

The wool of My sheep portrays its value to the sheep,
        portrays the image of the sheep,
        portrays the grooming of the sheep.

The wool of My sheep is of importance to the sheep,
        is of importance to the shepherd,
        is of importance as the climate varies.

The wool of My sheep is of importance in conforming,
        is of importance in blending in,
        is of importance at the drafting gate
                swung by spots and blemishes,
                swung by veins of love,
                swung by evidence which cannot be ignored.

The wool of My sheep determines ultimate selection,
        presents the health of the sheep before the shepherd,
        calls attention to the effort spent in preparation,
                spent within a courtyard of great cleanliness,
                spent in seeking the intent of the shepherd.

The wool of My sheep speaks of where they played,
        speaks of where they browsed,
        speaks of where they roamed.

The wool of My sheep speaks of whether they were dipped for hangers-on,
            whether they were crutched and tended,
           whether they were vaccinated against disease.

The wool of My sheep speaks of whether there was a history of delinquency,
                    a history of rambling in the thorns,
                    a history of shed blood in which the
                          fleece was washed to soak
                              in through the skin.

The wool of My sheep with the whiteness of purity,
        with the absence of stains which were removed in preparation,
        with the scent of the oil buried deep within the folds:
    testifies of a shepherd who took great interest in His sheep;
    penned them and protected them throughout the hours of darkness;
    led them and had them know His voice when calling for response;
    brought them to where the pasture was filled with nourishment;
    quenched their thirst in drinking from the waters of new life;
    guarded them from the wolves and those who would do them harm
                by invitation to the barren lands.

The wool of My sheep is a blessing in disguise,
        qualifies the obedient—
            in purity—
    to exchange their outer coverings for their gowns of life,
    to establish their treasure in safe keeping—
            from which robbers cannot deprive—
                as held in readiness for a coming birth.

The gowns of life are wonders to behold,
    shimmer and sparkle in The Sonlight,
    have decorations which reflect earlier relationships of identity;
    always move in Grace upon The Graceful,
    always speak in confirmation of grace accepted by the lives,
    always acknowledge the presence of grace:
        as the key which opens the threshold of the eternity of choice
                on exiting the grave clothes.

The gowns of life witness transformations,
    witness welcomes into new surroundings,
    witness the restoration of perfection of the being in The Presence.

The gowns of life are witnesses to the introduction of knowledge:
        of the past mortality;
        of the spirits' prior presences with God;
        of the flows of information;
        of the enhancements of the senses;
        of the upgradings of abilities within the new environment;
        of the changes in both scale and time;
        of the companionships within the residence of
                The Living God."

My Content Study Aid

A New Prince is Born

"A new prince has come unto a kingdom,
        has come unto a family,
        has come unto the expectations of the kingdom citizens.

A new prince who will abdicate his responsibilities,
        who will abdicate his inheritance,
        who will abdicate The Crown in Waiting,
        who will abdicate in sacrifice for the greater good.

A new prince will know the path to kingship,
        will know the way expected for him to tread,
        will know the future of applause among the streets of honour,
                among the streets of invitation,
                among the streets of endeavour and of praise,
                among the streets of approval and of
                          authority bequeathed.

A new prince is born into a seat of royalty,
        into a seat of history,
        into a seat already filled and overflowing,
        into a seat reserved for his succession.

A new prince is born into a seat which will not become a throne for his sole occupancy,
        will not become a throne where he sits alone,
        will not become a throne which bestows his inheritance
                as the vicar of My church,
        will not be entrusted with The Authority of God intermingled
                with the idol of freemasonry.

For as such arise in pride so they are brought low.
For as such proclaim so their mouths blaspheme.
For as such protect their secrets so they condemn themselves.
For as such acknowledge The Faiths of man so they abjure The Living God.
For as such confess their misplaced forms of worship so their figurehead is evident
                          to The Wise.
For as such participate in the deeds of darkness so they earn The Wrath of God
                          awaiting revelation."

My Content Study Aid

The Friendships of Man

"The friendships of man are often wary and unconciliatory under the strain
      of issues tied to health,
      of issues tied to wealth,
      of issues tied to stealth:
    where warning signs are not immediately apparent,
    where the loss is sudden and unforeseen,
    where an attack on rectitude is unexpected yet effective.

The friendships of man are not established lightly,
    are cautious in approach,
    are in retreat upon a hurt,
    are damaged by rejection,
    are intended to survive the grave.

The friendships of man are tested from many perspectives,
    are not affirmed by a handclasp of declaration,
    are not affirmed by a lie embedded in a memory,
    are not affirmed by a lack of attention when it is most needed.

The friendships of man are trivialised when centred on self-promotion:
        then have foundations built on straw;
    see the calls ignored while current;
    see fewer visits on the timeline of a friendship;
    see an initial friendship become but an acquaintance of the day.

The friendships of man can last a lifetime,
    can last a season,
    can result in mourning for that which has been lost.

The friendships of man can extend unto his pets of trust,
    can extend unto the animals for which he cares,
    can extend across the distances as families move or expand.

The friendships of man are magnified by love,
    are magnified as a history develops,
    are magnified as families grow together,
    are magnified through shared experiences—
      ones surviving through the storms so to flower
          in the sunlight of great joys.

The friendships of man see personalities interact,
    see characters of like interests,
    see kindred spirits resting at their ease,
    see souls drawn to one another
      because of shared beliefs,

because of shared goals,
because of shared knowledge of the past
and wisdom for the future.

The friendships of man answer a call for help,
answer a need for food upon a table,
answer a call where counsel is required,
answer a call for a season in a life,
answer a call for comfort in a loss.

The friendships of man are bound within the will of man to his fellow man;
are bound by the will of man to his loving God;
are bound through the three-way stranded cord
which weaves honour and integrity intermixed with love:
this as a standout sign pointing to the heavens
from where eternity is shared."

My Content Study Aid

The Aberrations of Man

"There are many aberrations in the life of man,
    many aberrations which are undesirable,
    many aberrations witnessing the need for correction,
        witnessing the lack of thought,
        witnessing the power of the peer group,
        witnessing mixed-up ethics as each proclaims his own,
        witnessing the lack of morals born of agnosticism
            in they who say they do not know,
        witnessing gender issues of the day which result
            in marriages in nothing but the name,
        witnessing the whispers of the killing for payment
            on the abortion tables of despair—
        where the surplus eyes of man are not permitted—
        where the acts are still seen by God together with
            His angels of the testimony.

The aberrations of man wield the sword of accountability over the heads of those
        whose silence confirms consent,
        whose silence denies dissent,
        whose silence is recorded in the present.

    The silence of man,
        in harbouring a silent spirit and a silent soul,
        will be to his great detriment at the judgment seat of God before
            The Great White Throne.

The aberrations of man are not glossed over by The God of man's creation,
        are not glossed over as if there were no sin,
        are not glossed over as if they did not exist.

The aberrations of man are not glossed over until the onset of conditions
            which beget the fall of grace.

The aberrations of man are not unduly repetitive,
        arise from freewill investigations which ignore the spirit's cry,
        should not comprise a habit in the making,
        should not see the soul succumb to that
            which is ultimately rejected.

The aberrations of man have a background of curiosity with wisdom non-existent,
        have a background seeking knowledge and experience,
        have a background closely watched by the angels when addiction
            is not on the horizon,
        have a background seeking approval of the peer group of the season.

The aberrations of man speak of the entertainment of man:
        of the facilities inviting man to play the many games
           of chance where the wealth of man is staked;
              of the publicans,
                the resellers,
                    the barns of bulk supply,
              being the enablers of the party—
              at the public houses,
              at the private houses,
              at the scenes of secrecy—
                  where alcohol is the menu;
        of the captains of industry producing leaf weeds packaged
            to invite their smoking as they rest upon the lips;
        of the tattoo parlours that disfigure the body of man
                imaged in the likeness of God—
            that designed to become a temple of The Holy Spirit:
            that testifying to the threefold acceptance of man.

The aberrations of man are as notches on a stick marking the progress of a life,
        are as a diary kept in secret of where the body chose to delve,
        are as washing on the line where the taint of yesterday still
                    lingers in the sunlight.

The aberrations of man should be perceived for what they are,
        should be perceived as urges not to be encouraged,
        should be perceived as best forsaken and amended
                before detriment is installed,
        should be perceived for correction with the spirit fully put
                in charge with oversight of the soul,
        should be perceived when functioning as a witness—
            when silence is not an option open to adoption.

The aberrations of man should not repeat on man within a cycle,
        should not become installed as a way of life,
        should not settle in as a seat of comfort.

Man should not nurture an aberrant soul which impacts
            on his welfare and standing before God."

My Content Study Aid

_____

_____

_____

_____

The Wonderment of Eternity

"The wonderment of eternity is a joy unto itself,
        is a feast for the eyes,
        is a symphony for the ears,
        is a dwelling place fit for The Stars of God.

The wonderment of eternity displays the works of God in their entirety:
        in their presentation of uniqueness,
        in their designs of grandeur,
        in their use of the full colour spectrum,
        in their originality of expression,
        in their ability to communicate,
        in their decorations of surroundings,
        in their sites of majesty.

The wonderment of eternity is the experience in store for The Family of God:
        of those who testified of The Son,
        of those who hosted The Holy Spirit,
        of those who greeted The Father in a prayer.

The wonderment of eternity builds on the eternal word to The Family of God:
        to those present with a thirst for knowledge,
        to those present with a yearning for wisdom,
        to those present with a desire for activity
                under the tutelage of the angels.

The wonderment of eternity stretches far and wide,
        stretches deep and high,
        stretches in and without.

The wonderment of eternity possesses dimensions for new senses,
        dimensions holding the history of man,
        dimensions displaying The Vistas of God.

The wonderment of eternity fills the imagination of man
        with new concepts and appraisals,
        with new structures and constructs,
        with new images and dispositions.

The wonderment of eternity fulfils the promises made to man,
        fulfils the curiosity of man,
        fulfils the wanderlust of man.

The wonderment of eternity upholds security of tenure,
        upholds antiquity within the present,
        upholds the disclosure of the pathways for the stars.

The wonderment of eternity encompasses the activities of God,
        encompasses the creation by God,
        encompasses The Love of God.

The wonderment of eternity is there for all mankind to claim as an individual inheritance:
        to claim within discipleship,
        to claim that built upon a sacrificial cross,
        to claim in a commitment to repentance,
        to claim via the redemptive reconciliation of man,
        to claim by shedding the entanglement of sin,
        to claim through understanding of The Grace of God."

My Content Study Aid

The Doorway of Mercy

"The doorway to eternity is soon to open in mortality,
        is soon to open prior to the grave,
        is soon to open within the sight of man,
        is soon to open for The Bride.

The doorway of mercy as it opens sees the shutting of the door of grace—
              with the fall of the sounding-board of faith.

The doorway of mercy as it opens sees the veil withdrawn from eternity
              with knowledge to the fore—
        as the bema of the mercy seat becomes exposed.

The doorway of mercy as it opens sees the entrance of The King Coming for His Bride.

The doorway of mercy serves The Multitudes at large,
        The Multitudes surviving the end-time tribulation,
        The Multitudes with faith and grace no longer relevant,
            with the new covenant no longer open to acceptance.

The doorway of mercy will be well trodden by The Multitudes,
        by those seeking mercy for their deeds,
            mercy for the accumulation of their sin,
            mercy for their spoken words—
                both in blasphemy and in lies.

The doorway of mercy is not repetitive in its access,
        is not repetitive in its functioning,
        is not repetitive in its assessments of validity.

The doorway of mercy is not subject to assault,
        is not subject to being violated,
        is not subject to proclamations,
        is not subject to relief from justice,
        is neither subject to appeal nor to parole upon a sentence that
              carries no injustice,
        is not subject to any other jurisdiction.

The doorway of mercy operates in the bounds of man's enlightened freewill,
        operates within The Edicts of The Lord,
        operates where lies are quickly known,
        operates where the intent of every heart is known,
        operates so justice is not imperilled,
        operates where the merciful are heard.

The doorway of mercy is numerous in its placements near the seats of justice,
              functions similarly to one another,

      evaluates and determines,
      rejects the dissimulators,
      hearkens to injustice.

The doorway of mercy examines the presence of opprobrium,
   examines those caught in a network of deceit,
   examines the outcomes where injustice may be a by-product.

The doorway of mercy knows and witnesses to the truth in matters of confusion,
      in matters with tiered applications,
      in matters inherited from the past
      where injustices were wrought.

The doorway of mercy testifies of the functioning of God,
   testifies of calling to account,
   testifies of wrongful death so brought by man,
   testifies within the morality of God,
   testifies where injury and violence had no right to be,
   testifies so the innocent may be reclaimed from their suffering—
      with reparation for when they were made a victim.

The doorway of mercy does not consider mercy where Grace is Already Present,
   does not permit infractions against the innocent,
   does not allow a victim to suffer from incapacitation.

The doorway of mercy receives such from The Loving God:
   receives such that justice may prevail,
   receives such that violence and dishonour may decline
      within the experience of man,
   receives such that righteousness with peace pervade
      The Multitudes of man."

My Content Study Aid

The Presence of Man

"The flood chambers of the heart know the mortal beat of life,
                        know when it was commenced,
                        know when it is about to end.

The flood chambers of the heart are protected and secured,
                        are reliable and entrained,
                        are consistent and effective.

The flood chambers of the heart are controlled and supervised,
                        are bespoke and sensitive,
                        are constrained and released.

The flood chambers of the heart support life within mortality,
                        seal completeness when the sands of time run out,
                        open the gateway to eternity after the time
                                            as set for preparation.

The flood chambers of the heart speak of the physical in contact with the senses—
                                      within the flesh of man—
                    maintaining life for the presence of man:
                            the shell of man,
                            the glove of man,
                            the body of man.

The presence of man includes spiritual connotations to the conceptual heart of man:
                                as to the intent of the heart;
                                as to whether it manifests
                                          in goodness or in evil;
                                as to the depository for sin;
                                as to the dungeon hiding places—
                                          thereby being in need
                                              of deep cleansing;
                                as to a metaphor for that seen as the
                                          outworking of the character.

The presence of man has sin hiding in his fingertips,
                hiding in his thought life,
                hiding in his offices,
                hiding in his libraries,
                hiding in his tools for accessing that for which he searches,
                                          that for which he finds,
                                          that for which he shares,
                                          that for which he stores,
                                          that for which he views—

when he thinks he dwells in privacy
of thought and word and deed.

The presence of man comes under subservience to God
when man displays self-righteousness,
when man is not meticulous with his tongue,
when man rounds off to ignore the rough edges—
the sharp corners—
the short cuts—
where shame so often hangs its coat.

The presence of man can see his fortunes change when he attempts:
to thwart The Will of God;
to hide behind lies constructed in a series;
to introduce deception to his armoury;
to scheme and plot for what he would wish
to keep as secret;
to infringe the laws of God and of man—
as stepping stones of infraction
to undue wealth or fame.

The presence of man can be such that he dishonours all he touches,
dishonours all he seeks,
dishonours all under his control,
dishonours all within a family:
by the stain of corruption implicit in his perception of leadership authority.

The presence of man can be as a renegade from God as man's freewill runs amok.

The presence of man builds or ignores his character,
builds or ignores his destiny,
builds or ignores his friendships,
builds or ignores his history of life,
builds or ignores his relationship with God,
builds or ignores the likely impact of Grace upon his being.

The presence of man is either the victim of the foe of man—
so destined for the satanic fold,
or the victor with The Son of God—
so destined for The Family of God.

So is The Truth declared;
so is The Truth to stand;
so is The Truth upheld,
so is The Truth not gainsaid."

The Restlessness of Man

"The restlessness of man arises from his perceptions of his life,
                from the lack of recognition of his own achievements,
                from the praise found wanting from his peers,
                from the absence of gratitude as signified by silence,
                from the erstwhile efforts expended without reward,
                from the confirmation of any significance attached
                                    to a life in jeopardy.

The restlessness of man is a sign of disillusionment,
        is a sign of diminishing self-worth,
        is a sign that all is not well within his soul,
        is a sign of a dampened spirit trampled and forlorn,
        is a sign which threatens the ongoing of life itself.

The restlessness of man cracks a nut and cannot find the kernel,
        plants a seed and does not see it grow,
        saves his income but finds his purse still empty,
        seizes on an inspiration though remaining incomplete,
        visits others only to encounter their gripes and groans,
        attempts to pay his debts and hopes vainly for a residue:
                looks finally upon his life and asks what is the use?

The restlessness of man is a ploy of Satan,
        is a trick within perspectives,
        is the undue emphasis of negatives without
                              the countervailing positives,
        is the dragging down of that which should be lifted up.

The restlessness of man can result from misapplication of his thoughts and deeds:
            the lack of worthwhile vision in his life,
            the non-ability to discern the turning points
                                  in life,
            not joining the adventuring,
                the journeying,
                      inherent in each life,
            not having a tabulated history of what has been
                      and done to which his spirit can recall
                              and his soul can refer.

The restlessness of man seeks progress in his life,
            wants to stamp on failure,
            needs to kick a goal.

The restlessness of man desires to hear the roar of approval so love can grow and cherish,

> so achievement can be measured by the pat
> upon a back,
> so he can smile when encountering the words
> well done uttered in sincerity.

The restlessness of man can be directed through the love of God,
> by a relationship with God,
> via the end-time journeying with God,
> in preparation to be The Bride of Christ.

The restlessness of man can be directed to be an overcomer,
> to be a friend of God,
> to be envisioned with a tasking from God,
> to be empowered with the gifts of
> The Holy Spirit,
> to become A Temple wherein The Holy Spirit
> dwells to counsel and to lead.

The restlessness of man can be but a stepping stone to the pathway of fulfilment
> in a life with God."

My Content Study Aid

The Resilience of Man

"The resilience of man surfaces in his attitudes to conquering and progressing,
                    to seeking and restoring,
                    to capturing and mastering,
                    to exploring and possessing.

The resilience of man is measured by his tenaciousness,
                    in his bounce back from near defeat,
                    in his recovery of will to discover ways around
                                            his difficulties,
                    in his adopting of new methods as
                                solution possibilities.

The resilience of man seeks the dispersal of information,
                shares knowledge mixed with wisdom,
                knows the headlines of discovery.

The resilience of man clings to a commitment,
                attacks problems with resolve,
                appreciates the value of resources,
                hearkens to counsel from the wise.

The resilience of man is birthed within the lighting of history,
                    within the past experience of man,
                    within queries for the future where expansion
                                    is sought—
                          to so meet the present onward needs of man.

The resilience of man rarely pays tribute to his creating God,
                rarely sees value in the honouring of God,
                rarely instructs his offspring in the ways of God.

So the would-be God of man waits upon The Multitudes:
                        waits and waits and waits and waits and waits;
                        with His offering of Grace,
                        with His offerings endemic in His promises
                                waiting for acceptance—
                        to be seized unto each heart.

So the would-be God of man has His seven angels hold lightly to their bowls:
                        with His contents of their bowls soon to be poured out
                                  upon The Earth—
                    within the time frame of The End-time Wrath of God.

So the would-be God of man watches and reveals Himself in love with grace
                                                    held high,

>   awaits and garners from the four winds,
>   insists on man's recognition of the divine sacrifice—
>   His Son interposed as the agent of reconciliation—
>   to so redeem man unto his waiting God.
>
> So The God of man is accepted as such by The Sheep within The Shepherd's flock.
> So The God of man adopts them into His Family.
> So The God of man seeks their preparation to be so numbered as The Bride."

My Content Study Aid

The Variance of Man

"The variance of man confirms stability of purpose,
                stability of existence,
                stability of development:
                      stability within the window frame of God.

The variance of man cycles across all aspects of his being.

The variance of man is for the benefit of man,
        is for the fellowship of man,
        is for the development of man,
        is for The Family of God.

The variance of man determines his abilities:
        his specialties,
        his weaknesses,
        his dependencies,
        his needs,
        his constructions,
        his food,
        his education,
        his reasoning.

The variance of man determines his skill set in facing life:
        his wisdom to learn from others;
        his wisdom in knowing when to share;
        his wisdom in protecting his advantage;
        his wisdom in the quest for happiness;
        his wisdom in evaluating resources;
        his wisdom in establishing his boundaries.

The variance of man is subject to long term trends:
        how he interacts,
        with whom he shares his bed,
        the parameters set for families,
        how he fills his days,
        his beliefs and superstitions,
        his faith and idolatry.

The variance of man causes friction amongst man,
        causes bloodshed amongst man,
        causes enmity amongst man;
        causes envy amongst man,
        causes pride amongst man,
        causes judgments of superiority and inferiority amongst man.

The variance of man is dependent on his long term positioning on The Earth,
                on his long term needs to cope with his environment,
                on his long term variance necessitated in order
                                        to survive.

The variance of man,
    safe in his own shell,
        has no authority either to question or to discriminate—
                on the basis of a history which is leading to survival.

The variance of man should create a sense of wonder and thanksgiving for the beauty
                                    of man there beheld,
        should create a sense of togetherness and belonging to
                          the fraternity of man,
        should create respect and admiration of how others have
                          solved their problems,
        should create kindred spirits as they all gather in unity of purpose
                          to worship their God of love,
        should create awe and wonder for and at The Living God—
                He who brings redemption with salvation
                      unto the understanding of man;
        should create an earnestness to accept the gift of grace within
                        its time set for acceptance.

The variance of man is not as a result of randomness—
                progressively acting as an agent of intelligence:
                progressively installing life with increasing ability and thought,
                progressively installing self-awareness and social order,
                progressively gifting thought patterns of originality leading to
                              new horizons,
                progressively endowing man with capabilities not then needed
                              for survival,
                progressively enhancing the intellect of man—
                    as he seeks to journey back to from whence his spirit came.

The variance of man perceives randomness demolishing back to componentry.

    So randomness never puts a footprint on a beach;
            never is the generator of life;
            never can design a construct of ultimate simplicity—
                                  as seen in the cell of life:
                fitted with its powers of reproduction,
                      of memory,
                      of duplication—
                      wherein man is seen to tinker with his claims."

The Choices of Man

"The choices of man are often not within The Will of God.

The choices of man are often not considered with eternity in mind,
                are often delayed until convenient,
                are often pragmatic to best suit the self,
                are often motivated by his bent for entertainment,
                are often selected with his purse in mind.

The choices of man vary on the day,
                vary with his emotions,
                      his feelings,
                        his outlook on perception.

The choices of man vary with his environment—
                          the heatwave and the cold spell,
                          the windstorm and the calm,
                          the downpour and the drought.

The choices of man should be tested at the footstool of The Will of God:
                              within The Envelope of Grace,
                        as witnessed by His favour,
                        as brought unto man's spirit,
                        as guided as if a lamp before his feet,
                        as affirmed by the counselling of his soul.

The choices of man cannot be aligned to The Will of God if such is never sought.

The choices of man cannot conform to The Will of God if there is no relationship
                                                                       of honour.

The choices of man cannot accept The Will of God if there is no fear of God embedded
                                                                       in the heart.

The choices of man may reflect constant repetition,
                may seem as if arising from the mire within a muddy puddle,
                may lead to failure of compensation as such becomes past due,
                may lead to shortness of breath as exertion places life at risk.

The choices of man can hamper man in his progress to a goal within mortality,
                can restrict man in his levels of attainment,
                can reduce man to a former shadow of himself,
                can impair man in restricting his coming and his going,
                can defeat man as burdens load him to collapse under duress,
                can withdraw from God as man's tongue vilifies the sacred
                                                                        and divine.

The choices of man are not labelled in order of priority,

          do not come presented subject to inspection,
          often show no accurate insight to the future,
          commonly are borne upon deception,
              are carried upon a lie,
              are made without due consideration where wisdom
                          is required.

The choices of man can vacuum up the dust with the dirt in the search for
                          scattered pearls,
          can drop the case for evaluation in the swamp of quicksand
                  from where it will not resurface,
          can be muddled in a bowl which swirls the fare beyond the reach
                        of common sense,
          can reach out for the unattainable in the overeagerness
                        of self-assertiveness.

The choices of man can set a victim on a pedestal,
          can splash a canvas with much paint,
          can drag a child into his manhood,
          can lead a youth into the sunlight of the father.

The choices of man can supervise and harness the wilful walk of man, can
          exemplify and master the righteous walk of man, can
          lead in developing the discipled walk of man.

The choices of man display his wisdom in achieving his showcase of mortality—
              the walking with The Lord on his journey home,
              the walking of return to The Family of God,
              the walking into The Son Rise which lights eternal life.

The choices of man can attest to the spirit's glow,
              to the soul in acquiescence,
              to the body preparing for renewal:
              to the walk within mortality which selects
                        an assured destiny.

The choices of man should ensure his walk on Earth is established as the precursor
                      of his walk in the company of God—
          with all God has in preparation to honour the very images of God
                      as dwell within their Temples."

My Content Study Aid

_____

_____

_____

The Surprises of Man

"The surprises of man fall upon him unexpectedly,
        fall upon him with suddenness of expression,
           fall upon him to overload his senses in the moment of application.

The surprises of man are varied and far reaching,
        are dramatic and minor,
        are impelling and major.

The surprises of man may be life changing and intimidating,
        may be awaited and appreciated,
        may be random and peculiar.

The surprises of man occur both night and day,
        occur both in fear and in appreciation,
        occur both for his welfare and to his detriment.

The surprises of man may be welcomed or rejected,
        may be true or false,
        may be expensive or tawdry,
        may be bright or dull.

The surprises of man can affect all aspects of his life,
        can apply to all aspects of his death.

The surprises of man can be amicable or distasteful,
        can emanate from the sacred or the secular,
        can bring happiness or dreariness,
        can cause exertion or relaxation,
        can quicken or retard the perception of time.

The surprises of man are conveyed by the presence or the absence of the senses of man,
            by the action or inaction of the senses of man,
            by the reaction speed which dwells among the senses
                            of man.

The surprises of man are sprung by Satan in usurping vengeance:
        are sprung where faith is difficult to find,
        are sprung on the dissonance of man,
        are sprung without relief in sight.

The surprises of man are sprung by God:
            when Faith is immersed by the commitment of man,
                    within the mortal folds of time:
            to enhance the fear of man,
            to highlight the gifts of favour,
            in bringing Faith materialised upon the body

before the spirit and the soul.

The surprises of man can make a heart beat faster,
              can make a heart appear to miss a beat,
              can make a heart be stilled.

The surprises of man evoke memories in need of grading,
                    in incidents worth discarding,
                    in recollections worth correcting.

The surprises of man have occurred down through his ages,
              will continue in his future,
              will startle him in the present of his enduring.

The surprises of man lead him to discoveries he might not have otherwise had,
              lead him to his turning points in life,
              lead him to an accounting with God,
              lead him to the understandings of God,
              lead him to the forbidden zones of man,
              lead him to sin without remorse,
              lead him to acquire a habit to his pleasing,
              lead him to seek the help of God.

The surprises of man often lead to a new beginning,
                    to the crossing of a threshold,
                    to the waiting arms of matrimony,
                    to the promises of surprise,
                    to the wonder of surprise,
                    to the miracle of surprise,
                    to the prayer curtain of surprise,
                    to the reconciliation of surprise.

The surprises of man are not the surprises of God.

The surprises of man are not the surprises of Satan.

The surprises of man are not the surprises of the onlookers,
              are not the surprises of the attendants,
              are not the surprises of the hosts.

The surprises of man are tempered by his attitude to life,
              are tempered by his wish list,
              are tempered by his character,
              are tempered by his will,
              are tempered by his prayers.

The surprises of man need to be reconciled with category,
                    reconciled with relevance,
                    reconciled with impact on the spirit and the soul,
                    reconciled with the welfare of the body.

The surprises of man are events of importance:
> carry messages which should be understood,
> impart knowledge missing from experience,
> inlay the chords of memory in preparation,
> introduce certainty in the presence of uncertainty,
> warn man of imminent attack;
> should neither be ignored nor seen as of little consequence
>> when the attention span is stretched.

The surprises of man come without prior indication,
> come as a drop of rain from a cloudless sky,
> fall on the head of man even when sheltered by a hat.

The surprises of man are at their best when originating from God:
> when serving the purposes of God,
> when conveying The Will of God,
> when landing on man for the benefit of man."

My Content Study Aid

The Perspicacity of Man

"The perspicacity of man is difficult to assess,
        is difficult to observe in action,
        is difficult when the thoughts of man are jumbled,
        is difficult when the intent of his mind is clouded.

The perspicacity of man serves him well when healthy and developed,
        when defined and used,
        when kept available for My Spirit's counsel,
        when attuned and accustomed to The Tongues
                of My Spirit,
        when accepting the frequency of practice to
                familiarize the gifts of My Spirit
                      in fresh situations.

The perspicacity of man cannot be borrowed or lent,
        cannot be stolen or bought,
        cannot be discarded or trashed.

The perspicacity of man is contained within the bounds of life of the spirit and the soul.

The perspicacity of man is not an echo of his intellect,
        is not a second thought,
        is not dependent on his reasoning,
        is not a function of his logic,
        is not a benefit of learning.

The perspicacity of man is a built-in adjunct within the brain of man,
        is active when needed,
        can be accessed with a mental query,
        can impart the way of progress to a goal.

The perspicacity of man is the capacitor of the spirit,
        is charged by My Spirit when counsel is received,
                when wisdom is imparted,
                when the gifts of My Spirit become
                      evident in action:
        as a discharge is desired and achieved.

The perspicacity of man manifests to the surprise of man:
        both in hearing and in speaking.

The perspicacity of man assists man in achieving his full potential,
        in his vacating of the vacuous,
        in the fulfilling of his destiny.

The perspicacity of man stimulates his growth,

>   assists in skirting pitfalls,
>   measures well before the cloth is cut.

The perspicacity of man is not as sitting on a see-saw,
>   is not as riding on a roundabout,
>   is not as travelling in a lift:
>   each returning back to the beginning which remains unchanged.

The perspicacity of man is his problem solving capability resolved
>   by a flash of inspiration,
>   by an aha of exclamation,
>   by the innate knowledge of the route to follow
>   for a successful ending.

The perspicacity of man enhances the resolution of a difficulty,
>   that which may not be immediately apparent,
>   that presenting still as a puzzle,
>   that seeking a solution within the scope of effort.

The perspicacity of man can seek the counselling of God,
>   can bind on The Earth so to be bound in Heaven,
>   can loose on The Earth so to be loosed in Heaven.*

The perspicacity of man can seek both the physical and the spiritual—
>   by sight,
>   by ear,
>   by tongue,
>   by nose,
>   by touch;
>   with the spiritual also by the transference of thought.

The perspicacity of man should be fine-tuned in preparation—
>   by the gifts of My Spirit,
>   by an awareness of these gifts,
>   by the use of these gifts within the reality of man.

The perspicacity of man should be able to identify with My Spiritual gifts of knowledge
>   and of wisdom—
>   as he encounters his fellow man—
>   as he relates to The God of Abraham.

The perspicacity of man is to enable the present understanding of man in his end-time
>   relationship with God."

Scribal Note: *Refer* The Bible: Matthew 16:19 (NKJV)

Perspicacity: The quality of having a ready insight into things; shrewdness.
Perspicuity: Clearly expressed and understood.
>   *Able to give an account or express an idea clearly.*

The Wayward Wind

"The wayward wind is not of God,
        shows no control for the benefit of man,
        shows no symmetry within its existence,
        shows no signs of having an objective other than destruction.

The wayward wind brings confusion where there should be sanity,
        brings distress where there should be peace,
        brings disharmony where there should be unity,
        brings up the past where it should be forgiven,
        brings turmoil mixing into the season of tranquility,
        brings the grief of man into the time of his mortality.

The wayward wind is monitored by God,
        is subject to the sincere prayer requests of man submitted in understanding,
        is tended by God when the present bounds as set are exceeded on a whim,
        is verified by God as to having the presence of intent,
        is limited by God when threatening to wreck the works of God,
        is quelled when the souls of man become the fodder of the day.

The wayward wind is as a storm within a nightmare:
        where the mare of the night ventures forth to attack the stallion of the light,
        where the hounds of darkness are baying at the scent of blood,
        where the stampede of terror is corralled by the coming light,
        where the cross is seen emptied of its functioning with the coming of
                        a new covenant,
        where the nightmare ends with the love of man standing on a golden
                        promise with a pathway to a throne,
        where the wayward wind of miseries screams and howls in torment as its
                        grasp releases that which was its captive within time.

The wayward wind seizes to torment by loss,
        seizes to frustrate the plans of man,
        seizes to rob of life,
        seizes to impair the ability to enjoy a way of life,
        seizes to inflict both worry and despair,
        seizes to instil fear laced with mourning,
        seizes to take and to scatter the constructs of man.

The wayward wind banishes and throws away.

The wayward wind visits and dismisses.

The wayward wind carries and despatches.

The wayward wind has its season of freedom;
        is soon to become enchained;

becomes as but a memory within the few who witnessed it:
to know the violence in which it thrived in all its days upon The Earth."

My Content Study Aid

Downsizing So Smaller Becomes Better

"Release yourself from that which only brings frustration.
                      Let it go and consider it no more.
Open the path of joy which speaks both to your spirit and your soul.
            Do not be dragged down by that outside your control or influence.
                      Set such aside for disposal in a trash can.

    Clean by selection your home—
            of excess which lingers past its date of use.
    Empty out the spaces which the past still seeks to fill.
                    Set a place for memories.

Be determined in evaluating need.
Be thoughtful in classifying wants.
Be considerate in the sharing of acquisitions.

Seek and sup at the table of My fare—
        where the gathering attracts your interest for the feeding of your spirit.

Seek a place where you can be at home,
        where the extraneous do not impact on your senses,
        where the thoughtful and the considerate share their life experiences with
                      both care and understanding.

    Now is the time to restructure the important things held dear to the heart,
        those which well-served the past,
            clutter up the present,
            have little prospect of future use.

    Do not dwell in the frenzy of the recent past,
        select and knowingly discard that of little use or application,
        keep that which My Spirit indicates as of worth within your family,
        do not change your mind moving discards to a pile for keeping—
            those which have served their purpose yet can now still taint both
                      the present and the future.

Be ruthless in selection that the sun may rise upon a smile,
            that the sun may arise with the blessings of the day,
            that the sun may arise with the assertion of My Spirit,
            that the sun may arise on a home of contentment in which the
                  necessary are well placed and accessible for use.

Be free from the enslavement of that which you drag behind you.

Be free from the bindings of the past,

from that which has been gathered and now just fills a void,
from that which presents itself with queries as to placement and so gets
moved again,
from that which no longer actively serves the reason for its purchase
in another place,
in another time,
in another season of your family both in growth and in
development with a right to claim.

For such is the way to contentment in the life of man.
For such brings the soul to bow unto the spirit.
For such brings satisfaction along the pathway of discipleship under the tenets of God."

My Content Study Aid

The Journeying of Man

"The journeying of man is divided into three.

The journeying of man is measured by man within his shell of time—
>>to allocate his experience to his past,
>>>to his present,
>>>to his future.

The journeying of man as measured by God is on a continuum,
>is described for man as a circle of completion:
>>of initiation and presence of his spirit with his God;
>>of transfer by birth into the realm of his mortality
>>>with his freedom of freewill,
>>>with the approachability of
>>>>his God in waiting,
>>>with the handbook of knowledge,
>>>>of wisdom,
>>>>detailing man's freewill preparation for his return
>>>>>back to the fold of God,
>>>with the sign posts of life events there to lead him home,
>>>with his second birth through The Living Water
>>>>which affirms his fellowship with God,
>>>with the gifts of The Living Loving God who accepts
>>>>the worshipping of man;
>>of his third birth from the grave into eternal life—
>>with honouring of the freewill choices of the spirit soul
>>>and body in the presence of God or—
>>with an eternal soul where the freewill choices
>>>>are respected,
>>yet are called to account despite the record of the warnings—
>>>for the ignoring of the protocols of behaviour
>>>established for man by The God of Justice and of Truth.

The journeying of man is so planned to bid him a welcome home,
>to bid him a welcome to the promises of God,
>to bid him a welcome to the place prepared for his life of light,
>to bid him a welcome to his companionship with God,
>to bid him a welcome to his dwelling place within The Edifice
>>of God.

The journeying of man within the plans of God
>>brings to pass the ultimate fulfilment of man,
>>brings to pass the bestowing of his inheritance,
>>brings to pass his future outside of time—

        where all the wonders of God are preserved for man
                both to visit and to view:
      with interaction as the key to the discovery of life.

The journeying of man is no longer to be constrained
        as within a bottle sealed to float in time,
        as pushing at the inside of a bubble unable to break free,
        as testing the fields of gravity where bounding becomes
                an environmental variable,
        as no longer restrained by distances as known to man,
        as no longer restricted by the learning of man,
        as no longer limited by the senses of man.

The journeying of man should be filled with anticipation,
        should be filled with preparation,
        should be filled by acclimatization,
    should be filled with the wonders of God awaiting their discovery by man.

The journeying of man welcomes man to The Threshold of The Stars
        with all they hold between them,
        with all they hold-in-waiting,
        with all they hold beyond the imaginings of man,
        with all they hold for the displaying to man.

The journeying of man would have won the hearts and minds of man
        if they had but persevered,
        if they had but been open to The Word of God,
        if they had but sought understanding of the full
                significance of The Cross,
        if they had but chosen to comprehend what
                a sacrifice was all about,
        if they had but been willing to accept the free
                offering of Grace to erase the pull of Satan.

The journeying of man is not limited by time,
        is not forever limited by his body of the flesh,
        is not limited by the strivings of man within his mortality.

The journeying of man can retain all his abilities in their mortal heyday:
        compounded manyfold by his spiritual presence within a new reality:
        as filled with capabilities,
            with knowledge,
            with beauty,
            with items which fill all the senses of man,
            with satisfaction,
            with achievement,
            with the guiding hand of God."

The Generosity of Man

"The generosity of man is not without reward—
            as the accounts of Heaven would be updated by his tithes
                          and fruits—
            as they may be gathered into the storehouse of The Lord:
            as the windows of Heaven illuminate the storehouse of
                          The Lord,
            as My Word is spread by My Servants drawing from
                          The Storehouse of The Lord.

The generosity of man may contribute to My fare laid upon My table:
            where The Multitudes of man may so dine and feast.

The generosity of man may pay the fares of man incurred by My servants,
            may pay the expenses attributed to their movements,
                    to their feeding and to their accommodation
                    both of the day and of the night.

The generosity of man can soften the responsibility
            of those who guard the purse strings of My church,
            of those who would balance the weight against demand,
            of those charged with administering the funding along
                  the guidelines established for My church—
              in meeting the needs of those who come before Me
                    in honour and in righteousness:
                    from their history with A Lamb.

The generosity of man forms a beacon in the sky,
            centres a spotlight before his footsteps,
            lights the trail he treads in righteousness.

The generosity of man can endow his blessings upon the grateful,
            can share more than he is asked,
            can know his treasure and where he would want it stored,
            can seek the affirmation of God as a relationship establishes.

The generosity of man does not close his hands upon a hoard,
            does not rejoice at an increase in his wealth,
            is wise to acknowledge the source from whence it came,
            becomes aware of to whom it should belong.

The generosity of man startles the unjust,
            surprises the greedy,
            can lighten the way forward for The Stars of God.

The generosity of man becomes familiar with the generosity of God,

           becomes familiar with the objective of his life,
           becomes familiar with the target which enlarges on approach,
           becomes familiar with the guidance and the directions of
                                              The Lord.

The generosity of man does not succumb to envy,
           does not become a victim of false pride,
           does not wait upon the liars,
           does not frequent the presence of the drunkards,
           does not place wagers on the tables weighted to select a winner.

The generosity of man should deal in Truth and Righteousness,
           should honour both God and man,
           should testify of his encounters and of what The Lord has done.

The generosity of man can surface at The Spirit's Counsel,
           can encounter The Voice of God,
           can carry a potential temple where e'er he goes,
           can prefer the light to the darkness,
           can be aware of the call upon his life.

The generosity of man becomes stable and selective,
           becomes equipped with wisdom built on the gifts of God,
           becomes fluent in his tongues,
           becomes pure in his speech,
           becomes a recipient of grace,
           becomes known as a son of God."

My Content Study Aid

The Escape of Man

"The escape of man from life within mortality is always demonic,
                              is always fuelled by soulish activity,
                              is always at the leading of the soul.

The escape of man does not select his destination,
              has no choice of where he lands,
              has no hope for a change of circumstance.

The escape of man surrenders life at the behest of evil intent,
                   at the behest of all hope withheld,
                   at the behest of the lie believed.

The escape of man has fully surrendered prior to his escape.

The escape of man is a statement of a journey into Hell,
            is a statement of defeat,
                is a statement of the power of the demonic inviting to a place where
                               the authority of God remains unrecognized.

The escape of man ends the eternal prospects of the spirit of man,
                refutes his opportunity initialized for preparation for a much
                                           grander plan,
                succumbs to the downward pressures which brought him to fall full
                          length upon The Earth with Satan's heel upon his neck:
       to thereby claim his soul as a trophy for parading through the heavens.

The escape of man does not follow a hallowed course of opportunities,
              does not follow The Son of sacrifice,
              does not follow an acceptance of grace.

The escape of man testifies posthumously through a lost soul
                      of where his own freewill can lead,
                      of the terminal damage rendered to his spirit,
                      of the engulfing of the second death which denies
                                  the existence of grace.

The escape of man verifies the closing of a one-way gate,
                verifies a repository which never became a temple,
                verifies a struggle which ended in abject failure,
                verifies the absence of that which can no longer be.

The escape of man condemns the loneliness of man,
                      the despair of man,
                      the separation of man into what man categorizes as
                                                   a failure.

The escape of man shows he did not seek,
> shows he did not find.

The escape of man shows life declared no value,
> shows life had its purpose hidden.

The escape of man shows the defeating of the function of the grave,
> shows the lack of understanding.

The escape of man resulted from the absence of wisdom,
> the absence of love,
> the absence of companionship:
>> where burdens could not be shared.

The escape of man can be occasioned by the false teachings of a few carrying
> great responsibility for their forbidden counselling—
> both by oath and within the morality of God—
> to bring about an end to life which impacts on the present:
> to so steal a likely heartfelt future place with God."

My Content Study Aid

The Vanity of Man (2)

"The vanity of man keeps him from his God of Love.

The vanity of man permits him feeding at the tables of many gods:
>> at tables where the fare is composed of the lies of man,
>> at tables where deceit is practised,
>> at tables where the truth is denied in the absence of integrity,
>> at tables where the offering plate is always to the fore,
>> at tables where there are no gifts from the salacious
>>>> and the greedy,
>> at tables which only serve the will of man.

The vanity of man feeds upon his pride:
> feeds upon the prowess of his self,
> feeds upon his dominance,
> feeds upon his striving for pre-eminence,
> feeds upon the greetings borne by others,
> feeds upon the bonding of the obsequious.

The vanity of man is ruthless in his pursuits:
> is thoughtless in his relationships,
> is thorough in preserving the portrait of himself,
> is pre-occupied with his presentation,
> always seeks the kingmaker among the powerful,
> always joins an enclave promoting his objectives,
> always discards the stepping stones he tramples on his journey,
> always sheds his compatriots who would seize the limelight.

The vanity of man is not pleasant to peruse when seen in excess,
>> when seen in the formation of a character,
>> when seen attaching the blame for failure by shelving
>>>> it on others.

The vanity of man places him at the forefront of a queue,
> places him where apologies are unknown,
> places him where conflicting lies are sprouting from his tongue.

The vanity of man befriends those who do not compete,
>> those who will not overshadow his being and his presence,
>> those who remain subservient in their modes of address.

The vanity of man is promoted by the enemy of man:
> is promoted right to the threshold of his fall,
> is promoted with recourse to mirrors,
> is promoted by exaggeration,
> is promoted by proliferation of stories without foundation,

        is promoted by the shallow man who would dwell inside,
        is promoted by the peacock who struts in the feathers of the day.

The vanity of man denies a direct approach,
        sees him sidling up to first ascertain the lie of the land,
        often sees a crony being sent before,
        often tosses thoughts on to a sounding board to test what
                                      bounces back.

The vanity of man is not a redeeming trait when promulgated far and wide,
        when dominant within a soul,
        when the spirit is silenced through coercion
                of the will,
        when a walk is tainted by that which should
                not be.

The vanity of man pre-empts a walk with God,
        pre-empts the seeking of God,
        pre-empts a relationship with God,
        pre-empts the acknowledgement of God.

The vanity of man leaves him with his favourite flavour in the milkshake of his gods,
        leaves him wandering to a destination which has never
                              been considered,
        leaves him without discernment of the gates already hanging open,
        leaves him content as he strays both in ignorance and pride.

The vanity of man masks the possibility of repentance,
        masks the proximity of The Loving God,
        masks a change in lifestyle which has never been on the agenda
                              as being desirable or sought."

My Content Study Aid

_____

_____

_____

_____

_____

_____

_____

_____

The Son Shines

"The Son shines on the livelihoods of man.

The Son shines with a light that is all His own,
        with a light which is not shared,
        with a light as a focus point for gathering.

The Son shines as a lighthouse to the lost,
        as a haven for the woebegone in both appearance and their souls,
        as a shelter in a season of risk to life and limb.

The Son shines through the gloom which settles on the weak of spirit.

The Son shines in illuminating the unrighteous.

The Son shines upon the desperate who know not which way to turn.

The Son shines upon the forlorn who are seeking help.

The Son shines before the humble who are familiar with the fruit of penance.

The Son shines in surrounding all His flock with His presence.

The Son shines upon the call for grace.

The Son shines before the throne of The Father.

The Son shines in welcoming the sons of God.

The Son shines in showing each the place prepared.

The Son shines with the confidence of The Holy Spirit,
        with the confirmation of the assessment of The Holy Spirit,
        with the ushering into the presence of The Holiness of The Father.

The Son shines where darkness no longer reigns.

The Son shines where the woman—
    with her arms held wide—
        skips and dances with the movement in the reflections on the shorelines
                                                of The Earth.

The Son shines for all eternity upon the beauty of His creation awaiting the inaugural
                            showing to His Bride of beauty—
                which has held the chalice of redemption.

The Son shines forth so His identity is not in question;
        so He fulfils The Father's plan for full glory in His leadership;
        so He enables all due for an inheritance to confirm their claim;
        so He summons those from whom there is an overdue accounting.

The Son shines before the ignored warnings coming to fruition of indictment—
                                          with sudden relevance of meaning.

The Son shines so The Justice of God is to be experienced—

attached to that which was long thought to have been forgotten.

The Son shines where the aggrieved are gathered—
                          in the presence of The Mercy Seat.

The Son shines forth in effecting the dwelling place of default long since indicated
                                                      to man:
                    where grace was never accepted—
                    where mercy was never established—
                            by and for those who passed them by.

The Son shines upon His Kingdom,
        shines throughout His Kingdom,
        shines within His Kingdom.

The Son shines at The Gates of Heaven where those who testified may pass.

The Son shines before The Throne of The Father where He testifies of those accepting
                                            Grace as streaming from The Cross.

The Son shines in welcoming before The Father all His adopted sons:
            all within the covenant of blood arising from His sacrifice of The Son;
            all who relate to The Good Shepherd and prepared to be His Bride;
            all who have been through The Refiner's Fire—
                            to no longer bear the wood the hay the straw."

My Content Study Aid

_____

_____

_____

_____

_____

_____

_____

_____

_____

_____

_____

_____

_____

_____

Beyond The Grave of Man

"Beyond the grave of man is a wondrous place to be.

Beyond the grave of man is visibility increased,
        is hearing increased,
        is sight provided with better definition.

Beyond the grave of man is the fullness of existence,
        is the fullness of disclosure,
        is the fullness of The Glory of God.

Beyond the grave of man lies the sacrosanct and sacred,
        the holy and exalted,
        the glorified and adopted.

Beyond the grave of man rests astounding beauty,
        rests the promises of grace,
        rests the gowns of life.

Beyond the grave of man lies all The Works of God.

Beyond the grave of man does man enter into the inheritance of God,
        does man enter into a new assembly of life,
        does man enter into the fun-time of existence,
        does man enter into the surroundings of the tongues of Heaven,
        does man enter into his place beside The Son,
        does man enter into the security of eternity,
        does man enter into all which is prepared.

Beyond the grave of man,
        over the threshold of Heaven,
        way past man's preparation,
        with reinstatement of his memory,
        through enhancement of his capabilities,
        by the completion of the acquisition of wisdom,
        as knowledge is endorsed:
    so man grows in his finished stature as decreed by God.

Beyond the grave of man lies the freewill choice of man,
        lies the destiny of divine accompaniment,
        lies the destiny of solitude's default.

Beyond the grave of man are the marvels of creation,
        are the signings of The Upright Sons of God,
        are the journeyings of The Stars of God.

Beyond the grave of man is time encountered as a servant,

                    is time deployed by will in a scenario,
                    is time varied with intent of application.

Beyond the grave of man does man explore the infinite,
                    does man view the showcases of the heavens,
                    does man follow in the footsteps of the handiwork of God.

Beyond the grave of man are the surprises prepared for man,
                    are the blessings of man,
                    are the environments opened up to visiting,
                    are the parklands of rest and relaxation,
                    are the instant movers which can send and receive man to and
                                        from his destinations.

Beyond the grave of man is the hinterland of God,
            is creation stepping through the stages of accretion and of storage,
            is the visiting place of understanding the process of creation,
            is the initiation resulting in the installation of life in all its forms,
            is the land of cradles where immaturity still reigns,
            is designed to be the stepping stones where maturity is sought,
                                is attainable,
                        is to be confirmed by God.

Beyond the grave of man lies the birthplace of new beginnings,
                    lies the concepts built on grandeur,
                    lies the possibilities for the scope inaugurated within
                                        the oversight of God.

Beyond the grave of man lies the infinity of scale,
                                matched to each endeavour,
                                positioned with great care,
                                has room to move without the need to jostle,
                                settles in for the long term view.

Beyond the grave of man occurs the place prepared for man,
                                in all its streamlined comfort,
                                in all its futuristic facilities,
                                in all its comings and goings,
                                in all its modes of travelling,
                                in all its myriad of destinations,
                    in all its scale of preparation never before seen by man.

Beyond the grave of man are the venues and the auditoriums;
                    are the mountains and the valleys,
                    are the foreshores and the inlands;
                    is the water in all its applications,
                            in all its places of residence,
                            in all its invitations to take part,

in all its partnerships with life.

Beyond the grave of man dwells those with knowledge built on Faith,
with presence built on Commitment,
with wonder and with truth built on Expectation.

Beyond the grave of man dwells the once newly birthed souls—
who accepted the seniority of the allocated spirits,
who lived and loved in righteousness away back in the past,
who honoured and developed their giftings of freewill,
who each promoted a mortal way of life in preparation—
as The Bride of Christ-in-waiting prepared to meet her Groom.

Beyond the grave of man are the delights of the arts and the crafts,
of the hobbies and the interests,
of the discoveries and the investigations.

Beyond the grave of man is the laughter of the ages:
the giggles and the chuckles,
the guffaws and the sniggers,
the single and the grouped.

Beyond the grave of man the pets are understood,
the pets can come and go,
the pets are not enchained,
the pets are free to choose,
the pets are enabled to mingle,
to select,
to change—
their relationships of choice.

Beyond the grave of man is the grand design of life,
of scope,
of influence,
of variety,
of presentation,
of size,
of temperament,
of recognition.

Beyond the grave of man there is an existence quite different from mortality,
quite different in the life patterns,
quite different where scheduling is not sought,
quite different when time is not controlling,
quite different when hunger is not driven from
the stomach,
quite different when the sun no longer sets the days,
quite different when under the behest of God.

Beyond the grave of man is much to do and notice,
                is much to take in and assimilate,
                is the scope and scale of environments unseen upon The Earth,
                          unseen with the tools of man,
                          unseen within the cosmos known to man,
                          unseen and unimagined within the reality
                                        as proposed by man.

Beyond the grave of man is the sublime and the ridiculous,
                is the all-encompassing Estate of God,
                is the inheritance of The Son,
                is the power-house of The Father,
                is the hands-on of The Spirit,
                is the development of eternity,
                is the creation of The Loving God for all He wishes
                                                to preserve.

Beyond the grave of man is the planned playground of The Stars of God,
                is the home base of the angels fed with much activity,
                is the landing place of The Bride after preparation for the take-off,
                is the call for which the fanfare will be heard,
                          for which the trumpet blasts,
                          for which The Bride should wait in readiness of dress
                                    with the jewels all safely set aside.

Beyond the grave of man there is happiness and unity of purpose.

Beyond the grave of man there is no mudslide to defeat.

Beyond the grave of man there is no waiting for occasions.

Beyond the grave of man there is no need to queue.

Beyond the grave of man there is no time clock to be stamped.

Beyond the grave of man there are no appointments to break.

Beyond the grave of man there are no times allocated for the intake of food or drink.

Beyond the grave of man there are no habits to be broken.

Beyond the grave of man is fullness of expression,
                is the mastering of language,
                is the obedience of the tongue,
                        the lips,
                    and the vocal cords.

Beyond the grave of man there is no ageing of the hair,
                              the muscles,
                              the bones,
                              the portraiture of self.

Beyond the grave of man dwells The Provisioning of God,

    dwells the intent of God,
    dwells The Edifice of God,
    dwells accountability for freewill applied within mortality,
    dwells the imposition of justice where there was no justice,
    dwells recourse for the victims and the innocent who were
                  beset by man.

Beyond the grave of man is mercy tendered to the hard-done-by,
        to the unfairly treated,
        to the victimized,
        to the poor,
        to the hungry—
  through a mortality where a life experienced power misplaced,
          authority misused,
          governance usurped,
          assistance not rendered,
          judgments unjust,
          gaol time undeserved,
          fines improperly administered,
          corruption of officials.

Beyond the grave of man is the righting of the wrongs—
    the suffering inflicted by another,
    the sexual distress not paid due attention,
    the looting and the pillaging,
    the stealing and the defacing,
    the blood oaths entered into by man,
    the tongues with curses and blasphemy to the fore.

Beyond the grave of man there is hope with grievances resolved,
    there is love with harsh words not encountered,
    there is safety where life is not threatened,
    there is plenty where no-one goes in need,
    there is citizenship awaiting within The Kingdom of Heaven,
    there is reunion where friendships are re-established,
    there is The Presence of God with all which is thereby implied.

Beyond the grave of man is the confirmation of The Teachings of The Lord Jesus
                  in mortality—
    with all which was gained or lost
       by the presence or the absence
            of Faith within Freewill."

Appendix

Prologue:

The Hubble Cross	170
Journaling and Notes (1)	171
Journaling and Notes (2)	172
About the Scribe	173

Epilogue:

Laminin	174
Reviews of His Books 2 and 3	175
The End-time Psalms of God	177

Prologue - The Hubble Cross M51A Nucleus

"The heavens declare His righteousness,
  And all the peoples see His glory." Psalm 97:6 *The King James Version of The Bible.*

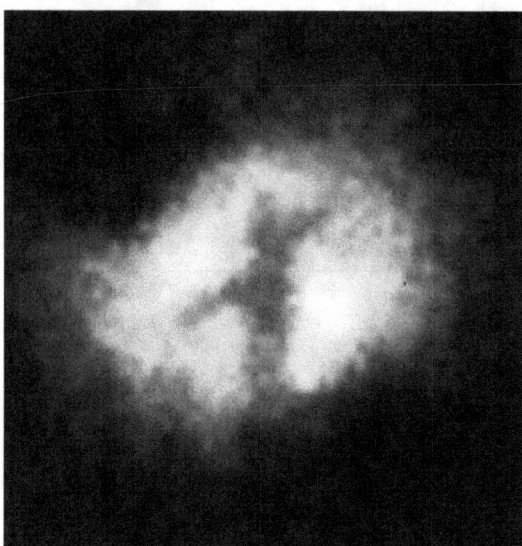

'The cross within the nucleus of M51A (or NGC 5194) indicating two dust rings around the black hole at the centre of the nebula.

The dust ring stands almost perpendicular to the relatively flat spiral nebula.

A secondary ring crosses the primary ring on a different axis, a phenomenon that is contrary to expectations.'

Technical
This image of the core of the nearby spiral galaxy M51, taken with the Wide Field Planetary camera (in PC mode) on NASA's Hubble Space Telescope, shows a striking, dark "X" silhouetted across the galaxy's nucleus. The "X" is due to absorption by dust and marks the exact position of a black hole which may have a mass equivalent to one-million stars like the sun. The darkest bar may be an edge-on dust ring which is 100 light-years in diameter. The edge-on torus not only hides the black hole and accretion disk from being viewed directly from earth, but also determines the axis of a jet of high-speed plasma and confines radiation from the accretion disk to a pair of oppositely directed cones of light, which ionize gas caught in their beam. The second bar of the "X" could be a second disk seen edge on, or possibly rotating gas and dust in M51 intersecting with the jets and ionization cones.
The size of the image is 1100 light-years.   Release Date: June 8, 1992
http://en.wikipedia.org/wiki/Whirlpool_Galaxy
http://imgsrc.hubblesite.org/hu/db/images/hs-1992-17-a-full_jpg.jpg
Credit: H. Ford (JHU/STScI), the Faint Object Spectrograph IDT, and NASA
http://hubblesite.org/gallery/album/pr1992017a/

Journaling and Notes (1)

Journaling and Notes (2)

About the Scribe

Updated 18 February 2019

Anthony is 78, having been married to his wife, Adrienne, for 55 years. They have five married children: Carolyn, Alan, Marie, Emma and Sarah and fourteen grandchildren: Matthew and Ella; Phillipa and Jonathan; Jeremy, Ngaire, and Trevor; Jake, Finn, Crystal, and Caleb; Bjorn, Greta, and Minka.

Anthony was raised on a dairy farm in Springston, Canterbury, NZ in the 1940s. He graduated from Canterbury University, Christchurch, NZ with a B.Sc. in chemistry and mathematics in 1962. He was initially employed as an industrial chemist in flour milling and stock food manufacturing with linear programming applications. These used the first IBM 360 at the university for determining least cost stock food formulations and production parameters. Later he was involved in similar applications on the refining side of the oil industry in Britain, Australia and New Zealand. This was followed by sales and managerial experience in the chemical industry.

The family moved to a Bay of Plenty, NZ, town in 1976 when Anthony took up funeral directing, as a principal, expanding an initial sibling partnership until the close of the century. Anthony acquired practical experience in accounting, business management, and computer usage (early Apples— including The Lisa).

Upon retiring from active funeral directing in 2000 and selling his interests, he then commenced the promotion and the writing of funeral management software for the NZ funeral environment. Rewarded with national success, he has now retired, in 2007, from the active management of that interest, living near some of his family in Hamilton NZ. Anthony was brought up in the Methodism of his father until his mid-teens, his mother's side was Open Brethren. He is Christian in belief within an Apostolic Pentecostal Charismatic framework of choice (since the 1990s) having been earlier in the Mormon church for several years. Thereafter he was in the Baptist denomination followed by finding a home within the Acts (Apostolic) church movement for some years, and now in Glory Release Ministries, one where all have made him welcome.

He and his wife, who has visited a number of Asian countries, have been to India in 2011, 12, 13, 16 and 18 on The Lord's tasks and have witnessed and participated in many miracles which befall His people and the multitudes.

His forbears, William Henry Eddy and Margaret Jane Eddy, née Oats, emigrated to New Zealand from Gulval, Cornwall, England in 1878 on a sailing ship, with a very slow passage time of 79 days, and with their three-month-old infant child, Margaret Anne, dying 21 October 1878 from 'congestion of the brain' on board the 'Marlborough' while en route to NZ.' The 'Marlborough' sailed London 19 September 1878, via Plymouth 26 September 1878, and arrived Lyttelton 14 December 1878 with 336 assisted immigrants. His grandfather, Alfred Charles, then but three years old, together with an older brother aged four, obviously survived the trials of the sea voyage to become a part of a family with a further eleven New Zealand born siblings all living to maturity.

Epilogue - Laminin

Photo via an Electron Microscope

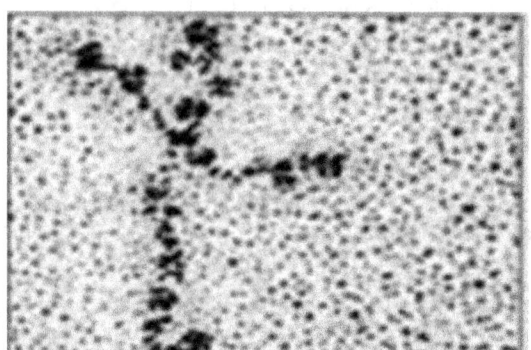

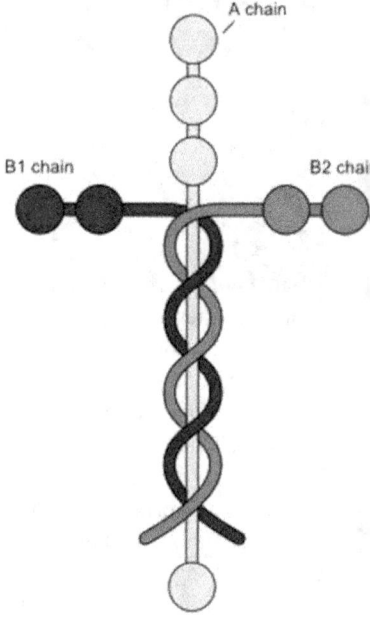

'Laminin is a protein that is part of the extracellular matrix in humans and animals. The extracellular matrix (ECM) lies outside of cells and provides support and attachment for cells inside organs (along with many other functions). Laminin has "arms" that associate with other laminin molecules to form sheets and bind to cells. Laminin and other ECM proteins essentially "glue" the cells (such as those lining the stomach and intestines) to a foundation of connective tissue. This keeps the cells in place and allows them to function properly. The structure of laminin is very important for its function (as is true for all proteins).

In a sermon, Louie Giglio asks how we can know that God will hold us together (which he infers from Psalm 33). He states, "That's really what we want to know today, and I'll tell you how you can know today that God will always hold you together, no matter what." Mr. Giglio then discusses the function of laminin (as glue), and its structure (a cross) in the body. He relates this to Colossians 1:17, which states (NIV), "He [Christ] is before all things, and in him all things hold together." His argument is basically that God designed laminin in the shape of a cross and gave it the particular function of "glue" in the body so that we can know (in his words) the truth that Christ holds all things together.'

Image credits: andrasik.oldpaths.net, (via Google search 'Laminin structure') & refer: http://www.answersingenesis.org/articles/aid/v3/n1/laminin-and-the-cross

Book Reviews— Books 2 and 3

Of Book 2— Three People are saying:

GOD Speaks to Man on The Internet

1st Reviewer: AJE
Anthony Eddy does it again! In this masterful collection of more than one hundred fifty poems, Eddy, speaking in his fictional role as a prophet of the Lord, presents a clever commentary on the synthesis of traditional Christian religion with modern-day technology. In this smartly-written collection, Eddy speaks extensively on God's love for His people, His willingness to save us from damnation, and the quirky "Website of the Lord", run by Eddy as a tie-in to this book series.
The Website of the Lord is also written in the same in-character format as the "God Speaks..." series, lending an extra air of verisimilitude to the entire affair. It gives the entire series the feeling of an Alternate Reality Game, and with ARGs being highly popular these days I applaud Eddy's forward thinking in combining Christian tradition with the ever-evolving modern world. I wonder if he has considered the possibility of a television series centered around his fictional prophet avatar? I'm sure it would be a big hit. But in the meantime, we'll have to make do with these books.

2nd Reviewer: JD
This book is different from others I have read. I do not make it a habit to read books in the spiritual genre but this is an exception. You will not be disappointed!
I enjoyed this book I must say. When I first began to read it I wasn't sure if it would keep my very short attention, but it did. The format used, making it look like poetry, is very refreshing to see, as personally, I had gotten used to the block style of writing. It keeps your attention by providing short and easy to read sentences, and you won't get lost as to what topic you're on because the author clearly shows you what they are talking about.
The book is too much for me to read in one sitting as I do most other books, because I did find it a bit overwhelming (but in a good way!). I managed to finish it only after a few days but in my opinion it would be better for the reader to divide it into daily readings. It would make a nice inspirational start to your day (or even at bedtime.)
The language used is fairly easily to understand, no big words or terms that would require a dictionary. Anybody who can read can benefit from reading this book.
I must include the part that although personally I am not a religious person, the book does make a strong case in building up (or rebuilding) your faith. Kudos to the author for creating this spiritual masterpiece!

3rd Reviewer: SS
Mr. Anthony Eddy's 'God Speaks to Man on the Internet' is quite an interesting read. It has been written from a new angle. A collection of a hundred and fifty poems, it has no plot or characters, but still is very engrossing for a person who is deeply religious. The

book talks of religion in terms of technology. This is the part I loved the most.
The chapters are short and sweet. Mr. Anthony Eddy conveys very deep messages and a lot of information in a very few words. That's what I appreciate the most. Although religious, his books, unlike others of the same genre, do not feel like long sermons. The poems are short and informative.
As I have said before, I loved the amalgamation of religion and technology. It is a rare perspective, and a good one, too. Kudos on that! I appreciate the forward thinking of the author, since most of the people have a common misconception that religion drags people backwards. Mr. Anthony Eddy successfully combines traditional Christianity with modern days, via internet, and proves them wrong, which, trust me, is very important for people like me.
I would also like to point out that the editing and grammar is almost flawless. Apart from some inevitable typos, the book is perfect from this aspect.
In the collection, Mr. Anthony Eddy speaks about God's love for His people, His willingness to save us from damnation and of course, the website of the Lord, run by Mr. Anthony Eddy.

Of Book 3— Two People are saying:

GOD Speaks as His Spirit Empowers

1st Reviewer: SB
This is, as we say in the United Kingdom, a 'marmite' book; meaning that you will love it or hate it. But I think those that hate it might just not understand it and miss out on its message.
I found the prose to be beautiful, and the messages in this book full of wisdom. If you are not a religious person, but a spiritual one, then you might appreciate this book in the same way that I did.
This is for quite a specific audience. I would recommend this book for a reader who enjoys poetry/prose and who also is religious or spiritual. I am not religious but am spiritual, so could appreciate this book with some open-minded ness. My main point of critique is that I feel if the name God had been used less, then the tone of the book may have felt more welcoming and inclusive. Reading this book did remind me a little of a sermon in church.
But with that being said I really did find statements in these prose that spoke to me a great deal. It is clear that a lot of love and attention went into this writing, that doesn't go unnoticed. My favourite chapters were 'The Aggravation of The Soul' and 'The Absence of God'. The messages in these chapters particularly could be applied to everyday life, regardless of belief in a God or not. Not being religious, I wasn't expecting to enjoy this book as much as I did.
Very pleasantly surprising and very thought provoking.

2nd Reviewer: JF

This is my second book that I have read by author Anthony Eddy. As with his first book this current book focuses on poems that are meant as conversations for the entire earth to hear. The book speaks on the coming storm for all of mankind. When I read the section on blessings of the faithful I felt these poems do relate to the theory of what I believe the world feels in regards to blessings and their effects upon us. From further reading this section I do understand a little more why we should be thankful for blessings. I feel author Eddy leaves no stone unturned in this recent book about God and his purpose for mankind in his message of the coming storm.

As in the first book I read from Mr. Eddy there are tons of repetition of poems and the words are constantly repeated. I believe the repetition is used to relate and focus on a clearer meaning of the poems and their messages. Since we all don't grasp the meaning of things at the same level I feel repetition is a good way for a person to keep reading until they can grasp the meaning of the message. I found the section on the soul interesting. The book outlines in great detail what the author feels the coming storm is meant and how it relates to God and all of mankind.

There's a section dedicated to both men and women, how they relate to God and his purposes for and about them. There's even mention on subjects such as: The innocent, righteousness, grace and mercy, speaking in tongues, Satan, and a whole lot of other subjects. Basically, something for everyone. The last chapter of the book is dedicated to the prophet Ezekiel. I found the coming storm poems very interesting and informative.

Books 1-9 of the parts of The End-time Psalms of GOD

	Pages	Total Words
1. GOD Speaks of Return and Bannered	416	87,061
2. GOD Speaks to Man on The Internet	498	122,349
3. GOD Speaks as His Spirit Empowers	272	65,494
4. GOD Speaks to Man in The End-time	248	38,920
5. GOD Speaks in Letters of Eternity	202	48,202
6. GOD Speaks to His Bridal Presence	326	78,183
7. GOD Speaks to His Edifice	514	122,516
8. GOD Speaks of Loving His Creation	280	67,234
9. GOD Speaks Now of a Seal Revealed	124	23,260

www.ingramcontent.com/pod-product-compliance
Lightning Source LLC
Chambersburg PA
CBHW050201130526
44591CB00034B/1660